# CELEBRATING DIVERSITY
## Through Language Study

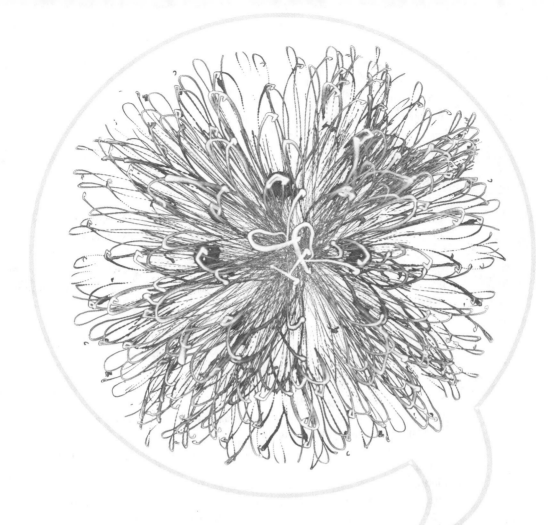

# CELEBRATING DIVERSITY
# Through Language Study

*A New Approach to Grammar Lessons*

## JEN McCREIGHT

**HEINEMANN**
Portsmouth, NH

**Heinemann**

361 Hanover Street

Portsmouth, NH 03801–3912

www.heinemann.com

*Offices and agents throughout the world*

**Library of Congress Cataloging-in-Publication Data**

Names: McCreight, Jen, author.

Title: Celebrating diversity through language study : a new approach to grammar lessons / Jen McCreight.

Description: Heinemann : Portsmouth, NH, [2016] | Includes bibliographical references.

Identifiers: LCCN 2016008922 | ISBN 9780325077895

Subjects: LCSH: Language arts (Elementary)—Social aspects. | Linguistic Minorities—Education (Elementary). | Multicultural education.

Classification: LCC LB1576 .M187 2016 | DDC 372.6—dc23

LC record available at https://lccn.loc.gov/2016008922

*Editor:* Holly Kim Price

*Production:* Vicki Kasabian

*Cover design:* Suzanne Heiser

*Cover photograph:* iStock/Getty Images Plus

*Interior design:* Shawn Girsberger

*Typesetter:* Shawn Girsberger

*Manufacturing:* Steve Bernier

Printed in the United States of America on acid-free paper

20   19   18   17   16   VP   1   2   3   4   5

To Linden, who I pray will grow up in a world
increasingly open to diversity,
in its many forms.

# CONTENTS

# FOREWORD

Language is never neutral. Even in a first-grade classroom, language embodies and reflects particular power relationships and sociopolitical realities. This point is powerfully rendered in *Celebrating Diversity Through Language Study*, a teacher's journey to self-awareness through language study with her young students. Walking what Jen McCreight calls "the tightrope . . . between celebrating language diversity and recognizing linguistic bias," this beautiful book tells the story of how a teacher can engage meaningfully with students on the many facets of language. While some educators may believe that the topics addressed in this book are too complicated for young children to appreciate, McCreight demonstrates not only that children *can* understand complex language issues but indeed that learning to do so can help young people make sense of the world.

Numerous educators and researchers have written about how a critical study of language can be used effectively with high school and college students. Bob Fecho's *Is This English?* (2004) and Hilary Janks' *Literacy and Power* (2010) are excellent examples. Vivian Vasquez's *Negotiating Critical Literacies with Young Children* (2014) is one of the few that addresses language study and critical literacy with the very youngest students. *Celebrating Diversity Through Language Study* joins these books, providing another vivid example of how teachers can unleash the power of language even with young children. This book respects children as capable of learning about the intricacies of language, from creating their own terminologies to getting how language is used in different contexts. By using a variety of texts, whether translation charts created by children themselves or literature with which they can identify, the author describes numerous models of student-centered and caring approaches for teaching young children of diverse cultural and linguistic backgrounds. Throughout the book, McCreight repeatedly makes the point that *context matters*. Where, when, for what purpose, and with whom one speaks all matter a great deal, an important concept for even young children to grasp.

If only this book had been around when I was a child in elementary school! Not only would I have benefited but my teachers would also have benefited. Rather than helping me understand how to negotiate language or celebrate my native language in school, my teachers instead taught me to be ashamed of speaking Spanish and embarrassed about my Puerto Rican heritage. I wish I could say that things have changed dramatically in the past half century, but in many ways, they have not. While it is true that the situation has improved in many schools—particularly in places that support bilingualism and biliteracy, and in others where ELL classes are an integral and important part of a school—this is not the case in other places. Language diversity, if not a taboo topic in many of our schools, is often ignored. The very act of talking about language is a powerful strategy yet, given the rigid guidelines for teaching language arts that teachers have to follow, talking itself is discouraged in many classrooms. Children who speak languages other than English or varieties other than standard English are still regularly told to "leave it outside" or even forbidden to use their language altogether in school.

Jen McCreight's first-grade students were fortunate indeed, for they were encouraged to explore language in all its forms. In the process, they learned that no language is a deficit language but instead that language in whatever form is a valuable and valid means of communication that must be cherished. Likewise, teachers fortunate to read this book will learn from the insights, perspectives, strategies, and many vivid examples included. Teachers of all backgrounds who teach students of all backgrounds will love this book.

*Sonia Nieto*

# ACKNOWLEDGMENTS

As language study is truly a collaborative effort, there are many community members whose ideas, inquiries, and energy contributed to what is written in these pages.

First and foremost, I wish to thank my students and their families, for so openly allowing me into their homes, their lives, and their language backgrounds. I have learned so much from them. I think often about playing basketball in their backyards, sharing delicious meals, and exclaiming over fast-growing vegetable gardens—I see the world differently for having known each of them.

I am also grateful to the co-teachers who worked with me on this project. Walter Avila, a dear friend and collaborator, taught my students and me Spanish, translated family dialogue journals from Spanish to English and back again, and came with me to visit families' homes. Dr. Katherine Brown brainstormed ideas and helped implement language study. Many other teachers, student teachers, and clinical students led small groups, held impromptu discussions, and visited homes to get to know families.

My own classroom language study was also infinitely enriched by university peers and professors, who exposed me to the research around code switching in early childhood spaces, helped construct and critique early versions of lesson plans, came to my classroom to take notes and offer feedback, participated in language invitations and family nights, and read multiple drafts of this work in its earliest stages. Dr. JoBeth Allen spent many hours with my students and me, learning about literature and language with us over many months and then engaging in critical reflection to unpack what we had done. Dr. Ruth Harman participated in lessons, offering ideas to strengthen the code-switching components of language study and posing questions regarding the impact of larger social structures on the language used and accepted by my students. Dr. Stephanie Jones challenged both my social justice lens and my writing of these events, pushing me to think more deeply about the many layers of experience and sociocultural connections existing within students' and families' responses. Dr. Jaye Thiel was a consistently brilliant sounding board and peer editor, helping me to solidify ideas and write about classroom events in ways that honored the students, families, and teachers who participated in them.

I am thankful, as well, that Konni Stagliano invited me into her third-grade classroom to work and learn with her students. In a very short period of time, her openness and natural curiosity about this work helped me to think more broadly about how to implement language study in upper-elementary classrooms. A master teacher, Konni creates a classroom community where questions and projects like those posed in this text thrive.

The editing, production, marketing, and design teams at Heinemann have also been incredibly helpful in turning my early ideas and chapters into the much more clearly written, visually appealing text that now exists. In particular, thank you to Holly Price, whose questions and insight were instrumental in focusing this work into something practicing teachers could easily use, and Dr. Sonia Nieto, whose early belief in these contents gave me the fuel to continue revising and editing.

And then there is my family. My husband's support has been critical to the completion of this work. I am forever grateful that he listened to me reflect on classroom events and provided endless hugs, dinners, constructive questions, and words of encouragement whenever I needed them. As is always their way, my mother, father, stepmother, and stepfather knew I would finish this manuscript even when I doubted myself. I hope they know just how much this meant to me and how motivating their belief in me is and always has been. Then there is my daughter, whose newfound use of words in her young world inspires me daily to continue thinking about the importance of honoring children's language backgrounds and experiences.

Each of these community members has a stake in this text, as the experiences we have shared, the conversations we have had, and the relationships we have developed all intermingled to create the foundation of language study. It is my sincere hope that the words in these pages do justice to the depth of the impact they have had, and continue to have, on this work. May we continue to learn and grow together.

# INTRODUCTION

Mack finished reading aloud an excerpt from his family dialogue journal (as shown in the chapter epigraph), a compilation of letters written back and forth between families, students, and teachers as a way to share our classroom experience. This week, we wrote about people with different skin colors, asking our families, "When do you see people that look different than you in the world?" Mack's mother, Natalie, responded, "We all have different skin tones but can be part of the same nationality." As Mack read her words in his clear, high voice, his fingers grasping the sides of his journal, it was as if she were there in the room with us.

Dear family,
Some skin color is the same. But skin color is different. I have skin color. Everybody has skin color.

As was our classroom practice, when Mack finished reading, he looked at his classmates and inquired, "Does anyone have any questions or connections?"

Hector's hand shot into the air.

"Hector?" Mack called.

Hector's eyes immediately filled with tears. The mood in the room became tense, as we all realized something was wrong, *really* wrong, with Hector.

These students and I had worked and learned together for their kindergarten and first-grade years, and we cared deeply for one another. I frantically tried to link bits and pieces of Hector's family and home life to Mack's journal but was unable to identify an immediate connection between Natalie's reference to different skin tones and Hector's mother, father, five-year-old sister, and infant brother.

"Someone called my house yesterday," Hector began. "He said that my family shouldn't be here because we don't speak good English, and that we should move back to Mexico. We're moving in February."

My thoughts began to whirl with phrases like "It's going to be OK" and "I know that must be so hard." Instead of saying them out loud, however, I sat silently, realizing that language, a topic that had been at the crux of our classroom learning all year, was failing me.

After a moment of silence, somehow I spoke, if for no other reason than to not allow Hector to continue facing his unusually quiet friends.

"Hector, your home is *here*. You have a home in Mexico, but you have a home *here*." I connected Hector's pronouncement to Mack's journal entry, adding, "You know those people whom we've talked about who thought people with different skin colors shouldn't be together?"

Michael nodded vigorously, raising his hand and stating, "Yeah, it's just like that. Sometimes people don't like different languages, just like they didn't like different skin colors."

Christopher rose from Rest Stop (our classroom spot for engaging in contemplation, deep breaths, and quiet time to recover from stomachaches or homesickness). He quickly wound his way around rectangular tables and stray chairs and raised his hand even before he sat down.

The rest of the class sat wide-eyed as Christopher said, "Hector is my best friend. I don't want him to move! I came over here because he is sad and I want to hug him. I don't want him to move!"

Christopher swiftly rose and gave Hector a long, tight hug. I was thankful for the simple brilliance in this action. "We *all* love you very much, Hector. No matter what, you have a family in this classroom." Hector nodded bleakly, tears still on his face.

Inwardly, I wondered how Hector had heard this conversation, what threats had been made to his Spanish-speaking family, and whether I should contact anyone from his home to ask for some clarification.

Outwardly, I did the only thing I could think to do.

We had a hugging party.

We would be fine.

Right?

This story highlights the tightrope my students and I walked between celebrating language diversity and recognizing linguistic bias. While Hector's story was the first, students periodically told friends and teachers about a "bad man" who called the homes of "all people who spoke Spanish and who were from Mexico" to tell them to move back, "unless they had papers." Families prepacked bags and mothers told their children they might be moving to Canada. The possibility of these pending moves took up conversational space from morning meeting until recess.

Each time a single child shared, others made our classroom "connection" sign with their hands, their thumbs and pinky fingers held high to indicate they had encountered something similar in their homes. Their experiences made the anti-immigration legislation sweeping across the country come alive.

## Language Study

Students need the space and time to share stories like these, and when they enter a classroom, they deserve to know their language backgrounds will be honored, not silenced. Language study does just that: it honors students' home languages. Language study, in its simplest form, is a student-centered approach to grammar study. This approach has two main components: (1) to teach students how to negotiate the language they use based on *context* and (2) to build on *background knowledge* to make the study of words relevant for all children (see **Figure I.1**). Teachers can use it exclusively to teach grammar, or teachers can choose to embed language study into an already existing grammar curriculum.

For example, while completing grammar worksheets or diagramming sentences, students and teachers can discuss the contexts in which knowing these rules might be most useful. While learning the standardized English rule for the use of *is* versus *are*, a teacher could ask, "Where have you heard people using *is* and *are* in this way?" or "Would you be more likely to apply this rule when you are speaking with your friends on the playground or while giving a speech or writing an essay? Why?"

The earliest goal of language study is to bring together children's home and school language backgrounds. Students begin the year discussing and comparing and contrasting the language they already use with friends, family, and other adults and peers in settings like school. They create their own terminology (or metalanguage) to discuss the switches they make when speaking in a variety of contexts and with a variety of people. With this foundation, children begin to view their language backgrounds as important and connected to the school study of words. Teachers identify

| Language Study Is . . . | Language Study Isn't . . . |
|---|---|
| a student-centered approach to studying language in use at increasingly in-depth levels | a set of prescriptive lessons to follow |
| based on the needs of the teacher and the students | one size fits all |
| an effective way to engage students across content areas | an add-on |

FIGURE **I.1**
What Is Language Study?

mentor texts (either excerpts from children's literature or snippets of real conversations heard throughout the day) from which they can pull interesting examples of language for closer examination. Students begin to identify the purpose and function of conversations with a variety of people and in a variety of contexts (for example, with friends versus with principals or talking around the dinner table versus speaking at an assembly).

## The Importance of Integrating Language Study into Our Curriculum

As the story about Hector makes clear, children's language is an intensely personal part of their lives, intertwined with their families, cultures, and experiences. As such, all students and teachers in the elementary grades, no matter their linguistic backgrounds, would benefit from a student-centered approach to language study. In fact, I would go so far as to say students and teachers *need* to incorporate some version of language study into their English language arts instruction, as a way to reclaim and *recontextualize* a subject area that is all too often taught without individual students and unique backgrounds in mind.

In all other subject areas, teachers acknowledge as best practice the necessity of building on prior knowledge. They comb the library shelves for books based on their students' interests and reading levels. They encourage children to write personal narratives when learning the concept of beginning, middle, and end. In social studies, teachers create businesses with products to sell to solidify the concept of goods and services. Even in mathematics, teachers create word problems that use their students' names or focus on topics in which the children are interested. We should approach the study of how words work in the world, then, in a similar manner.

Too often, the most critical stakeholders in education (students, teachers, and families) receive conflicting messages that undermine their ability to engage in meaningful English language arts learning. On the one hand, districts spend millions of dollars on standardized programs for language and literacy, complete with teacher scripts, grammar worksheets, discussion guides, and previously selected children's literature. These districts often expect their teachers to take these programs at face value, to replicate them because they are "scientifically based" and foolproof. Many times, teachers' schedules are mapped out prior to the beginning of the school year, so that they are being told not only *how* to teach content but *when*. Students and families are expected to fall in line, while rarely being asked for their perspectives or input. The dissemination of these programs undermines the knowledge of the teacher, the individuality of each student, and the autonomy of families, at the cost of authentic connections between home and school.

On the other hand, educators are reprimanded for letting students fall through the cracks, for not reaching all children through individualized instructional methods. Families read and hear that they are not involved enough in their children's schooling. Students are written about as passive learners who need to take more responsibility for their own learning.

Teachers know in their guts (and they are supported by the literature!) that children must feel invested in school to thrive there. They must believe school is interested in and values their home lives to meaningfully engage in curricular content. Further, families whose linguistic and cultural backgrounds are different from those prized in schools feel isolated when they are *told how* to help their children learn, rather than being *invited to* the curricular table as partners.

There is no more personal topic that bridges the divide between home and school than language. Children live their home languages, experiencing them through lullabies and jokes and family stories, from the time they are born. Upon entering school, those who speak languages and dialects other than standardized English (Hudley and Mallinson 2011) are often asked to disconnect from them in favor of mastering the "correct" way of speaking. Rather than building on students' prior knowledge, celebrating linguistic diversity and the wonder inherent in multiple ways of speaking, grammar programs all too often silence home languages and dialects; in the process, they also silence children's lullabies, jokes, and family stories.

It is because of the intimate connection children and families have to their home languages that I believe it is essential for teachers, schools, and districts to reenvision language study. By linking language study to children's backgrounds, and by empowering teachers, students, and families to become actively engaged in this work, we will begin to shrink the disconnect so many children feel from school.

## The Benefits of Language Study

When I began language study with my first graders, I had been teaching for seven years, in the thick of the standardized testing movement, and my students' linguistic backgrounds rarely matched the grammar found on these exams. I was passionate about teaching students how to code switch, or how to alternate between dialects or languages depending on the context of a situation (Genishi and Dyson 2009). I originally focused on this largely because language questions on standardized tests measured only a students' ability to speak standardized English (Hudley and Mallinson 2011), the dialect spoken on television, in most books, and in workplaces around the country. While I believed that all children's home languages should be welcomed into written and spoken classroom discourse, the students I taught needed to know how to speak the language of power (Delpit 1995), and it was my responsibility to teach it to them. I agreed with Knapp and Watkins, who stated, "The more we know about what language is doing, the greater chance we will have to make it work for us as speakers and writers" (2005, 35).

Literature on language diversity supports this view. African American scholars such as Lisa Delpit (1995) and bell hooks (1989) have asserted their belief that all educators should teach their students how to speak standardized English, because they are at a distinct disadvantage if they use other home dialects or languages to write term papers, apply for a job, or construct a college essay. Delpit and hooks both cite conversations with African American families who agree with them, lamenting the fact that well-meaning European American educators often do not teach standardized English because they don't want their students to feel bad about their home languages. Historically, researchers have found that adults oftentimes consider a child who speaks African American Vernacular English (AAVE) or Spanish as less intelligent than a child who speaks standardized English (Delpit 1995; Nieto 2002). Such prejudice follows these children into their teenage and adult years.

My students' experiences correlated with this larger body of scholarship. When I informally analyzed a first-grade language arts achievement test created by my school district, I was shocked to find that, although only one of the elements embedded in our state standards discussed grammar (subject-verb agreement), 20 percent of the district's test questions were language related. Of this 20 percent, which consisted of ten multiple-choice questions, 80 percent explicitly asked, "Which word *best* completes the sentence?" The creators of the test decided the best response was the answer that followed the rules of standardized English. Therefore, in the test's gross overrepresentation of one element covered in the first-grade standards, our district emphasized the weight of standardized English. It also made clear I needed to expose my linguistically diverse students to this powerful language. I found Hicks was correct when she stated, "Children must learn not only what to say and how to say it, but also when to say it"

(1995, 64) when learning how to negotiate the discourse of school. So, I made this exposure to standardized English my early focus.

Scholars such as Delpit (1995) and Nieto (2009) have wrestled with the best way to teach students standardized English, contemplating concrete ways to push back against the inconsistency present in a world that insists children must conform before they can stand out. As Linda Christensen, a European American who taught for thirty years in the inner city of Portland, Oregon, asserted,

> we must teach our students how to match subjects and verbs, how to pronounce lawyer, because they are the ones without power and, for the moment, have to use the language of the powerful to be heard. But, in addition, we need to equip them to question an educational system that devalues their life and their knowledge. If we don't we condition them to a pedagogy of consumption. (1996, 212)

In my earliest years of teaching, when I taught my students to code switch from their home languages and dialects to standardized English, I considered what such calls to action would look and sound like in my own classroom.

I began to realize that linguistic discrimination, whether presented through the questions on a standardized test or simply through teachers' lowered expectations, was common (Dyson 2001b; Hudley and Mallinson 2011; Schleppegrell 2010). My students and I were up against a wall—a wall made of mandates and societal pressure. I felt powerless to change the approach to grammar study that had so strongly embedded itself in schools, so I focused on activities that helped my young students understand the *relevancy* of learning how to speak standardized English (Gebhard, Harman, and Seger 2007). Similar to teachers in Heath's study *Ways with Words* ([1983] 1996), I used language detective journals to study words we used in different contexts. Based on the work of Wheeler and Swords (2004), my students and I created translation charts to practice moving back and forth between home and school languages. Similar to studying mixed-genre texts (e.g., historical fiction, a children's book with rhythm and rhyme), we discussed the overlap between forms of language we used in different contexts (Knapp and Watkins 2005). We focused on the importance of function and relevance in the midst of an educational environment that, at the institutional level, ignored the possibility or presence of linguistic diversity.

Yet I remained unsatisfied, as simply reconstructing the status quo does little to change it. Though I was on the lookout for opportunities to engage in action-oriented language work, I never knew just how much to delve into discussions on power structures and prejudice with six-year-old children.

## Learning from Home Lives and Families

It was during my seventh and eighth years as a teacher, as I got to know the students in Hector's class, that I identified the gap I had intuitively felt. My students and I lived and learned in a southern university town, with 99 percent of our school community receiving free or reduced breakfast and lunch and most living in a rural area. I often heard roosters crowing on my way to work, and children whose families were from Mexico and South America (70 percent) mentioned in passing how they slaughtered chickens and harvested gardens in the backyards of their small, brightly painted trailers. Most of the African American (25 percent) and European American (5 percent) students resided on quiet, tree-lined streets lacking sidewalks, where they played in large grassy areas and waved to neighbors riding by on bicycles, far removed from the farms.

I was a European American female in my late twenties. I had lived a middle-class existence all my life. On paper, I was quite different from the students and families with whom I was working.

I began to realize that in my earlier work, students' most relevant linguistic models, the adults in their lives, were largely *under-* or even *un*represented in our discussions around code switching and the contextualization of language use. Therefore, asking these families to engage in conversations about language was essential; it was how I would learn the ways communication played out in their lives. I wished to better understand these families as individuals, rather than simply as part of a larger cultural group, so it was crucial that we cocreated a classroom where they felt we authentically represented their home lives. As Anne Haas Dyson stated, "the larger processes of children's lives always penetrate the space of schooling, although . . . they are not always recognized, acknowledged, or responded to" (2001a, 15), and it became my focus to build our language study on these immensely rich ties.

Research has continually shown that families bring a wealth of knowledge and resources to their children's classrooms. When school curricula honor, support, and expand this knowledge, they create vast opportunities for more inclusive linguistic curricula (Allen 2010; González, Moll, and

Amanti 2005; Henderson et al. 2007). My prior experiences with these families told me that they had a deep-seated interest in supporting their children in whatever ways possible, and it was my responsibility to invite their knowledge and experience into our classroom.

The teacher–researcher team of Solsken, Willett, and Wilson-Keenan (2000) wrote about their experiences in creating open spaces for hybrid, multilayered pedagogies to emerge through dialogue, and their honest recounting of this experience greatly affected my thoughts on home–school partnerships. They stated:

> By positioning the children and their families as hosts and teachers, we hoped a new sense of agency would emerge. By positioning ourselves as learners and interrogating our own practices and ideologies, we hoped to learn how to construct a more democratic, multicultural pedagogy. (181)

In other words, if I wanted to open up these partnerships, I had to remember that this was not my show. The goals of our language work could not be mine alone. The route we would take to reach these goals could not consist only of my ideas. A collaborative language study would emerge only through dialogue and a focus on hearing, understanding, and learning from one another (Freire 1972).

I began to open up our classroom doors in ways I had not done before. And in the midst of this, critical realizations about language use in classrooms began to emerge. We shifted the conversation in unexpected ways as we implemented home visits, interviews, family dialogue journal entries focused on language use, and invitations to share language (Allen 2007). We began by primarily considering the contexts in which we spoke, and we eventually moved toward contemplating the linguistic discrimination that Hector and others faced. With the support and input of our families, we identified possibilities for action. Our initial fear and uncertainty became an opportunity for educating others.

## How This Book Is Organized

There are building blocks to language study (see the graphic that follows). You can incorporate this model fully into your classroom; you can choose to try out the first step or two; or you can choose to create and implement some variation of the activities and projects to best fit your students' needs, your comfort level, and your school environment. In each chapter you'll find

| **1 Extending Invitations**<br>■ Engage students in language study by thinking together about word choice.<br>■ Assess prior knowledge. | **2 Creating Translation Charts**<br>■ Translate words and phrases based on context.<br>■ Categorize and document. | **3 Identifying a Problem**<br>■ Identify language problems and explore challenges.<br>■ Create a plan. |
| --- | --- | --- |

- a description of the building block;
- specific examples from my first-grade classroom and a third-grade classroom;
- a chart that offers details and suggestions for each building block across grades K–6; and
- ideas for strengthening family–school partnerships.

Each building block can stand on its own and is malleable enough to be reenvisioned and reformatted. I present them in sequential order, as they build on one another.

*Chapter 1. Extending Invitations: Introducing a Language Study*

Based on the work of Van Sluys (2005), invite your students to explore their use of language. In small groups, the children might examine photographs, children's literature, video clips, or advertisements and discuss how people might be using language in each context.

*Chapter 2. Creating Translation Charts: "That's Not My Book Talk!"*

Extending the work of Heath ([1983] 1996) and Wheeler and Swords (2004), you and your students can use charts as a tool to discuss how context influences word choice.

*Chapter 3. Language Problem Solving: Identifying a Problem and Creating a Plan*

As your discussions about language use increase, you and your students may recognize that not all ways of speaking are validated in spaces outside your classroom (e.g., libraries and library books, office buildings, on television). Responding to this, you will engage in a language-based form of creative problem solving (Treffinger and Isaksen 2005) by first working together to identify a problem and then mapping out a plan to address it.

| **4** **Taking Action** | **5** **Celebrating Language** | **6** **Reflecting** |
|---|---|---|
| ▪ Outline an action plan.<br>▪ Consider standards and content alignment.<br>▪ Identify resources.<br>▪ Carry out the plan. | ▪ Plan a celebration.<br>▪ Share with family, school, and the larger community. | ▪ Conduct formative assessment.<br>▪ Study context.<br>▪ Seek progression from abstract to concrete.<br>▪ Make sure power is shared. |

*Chapter 4. Language Problem Solving: Taking Action and Reaching Beyond the Classroom Walls*

> Once you identify a real-world problem and create a plan to address it, you will take action. Your language-oriented project will be unique to your students and their linguistic backgrounds and experiences. Examples from the classroom will help you envision how this might play out in your classroom.

*Chapter 5. Celebrating Language: Sharing with Your Community*

> After engaging in a variety of activities and discussions around language in context, share what you have learned with the community. You can invite family, school, and community members to share in the celebration.

*Chapter 6. Reflecting: Looking Back to Move Forward*

> After you complete a language study, it's time to reflect. Take time to consider how language study affects academic performance, student and family engagement, and your approach to teaching grammar and language.

# EXTENDING INVITATIONS |

## Introducing a Language Study

Dr. Ruby, a university professor and volunteer, and Mack sat around a stack of photographs while other children excitedly chattered about language use all around them.

Pointing at a photograph of five children on a playground (see **Figure 1.1**), Mack asked, "Are these people speak different than this person?" first touching the four children on the left and then the one on the right.

Ruby encouraged him. "So you're saying they speak differently? Now that's very interesting. Why do they speak differently?"

"Ummm." Mack thought for a moment. "Because they have different skin colors?"

FIGURE **1.1**

"Oh," Ruby said, nodding, "because they have different skin colors. OK. So what do you think they speak in this one?"

"Like I'm talking," Mack continued. "You don't have the same English as me. But . . . I don't have the same English as you."

"Right," Ruby agreed in her Irish accent. "Yeah. Very good."

Mack, an African American student who sometimes spoke African American Vernacular English (AAVE) at home, was an incredible conversationalist. He had a thoughtful demeanor when discussing ideas that were important to him, such as the work of Wangari Matthai or Martin Luther King Jr. "Let me say somethin' about that" was his characteristic phrase, and he spoke with authority. His mother once told me, "Mack was talking like he just knew what he was doing, like he was just all together. And I said, that's Mack. That's Mack. That's just who he is."

Mack's seriousness and authority, his belief that "he was just all together," was evident in his responses to Ruby. In the midst of the noisy inquiries, the shuffling of newspaper ads and book pages, Mack and Ruby engaged in this short conversation about the relationship between skin color and language. This exchange illustrates Mack's understanding of language diversity. We had not previously discussed "different English," as he called it, but he recognized the difference between his and Ruby's ways of speaking. The fact that Mack believed language could vary based on skin color spoke to his understanding of dialect, even if he could not describe it as such. Language study helps all students develop a nuanced understanding of language.

## Language Invitations

The first building block in a language study is the language invitation. Its primary purposes are to

1. *engage* your students in studying language by opening up a conversation about how they use words daily and
2. give you the chance to *assess* their prior knowledge and determine appropriate next steps.

Dyson and Genishi stated, "We appropriate words from a shared linguistic repertoire to name and narrate our experiences. In this way, language is both a repository of cultural meanings and a medium for the production of meaning in everyday life" (2005, 5). The language invitation encourages teachers and students to begin a discussion about how they name and narrate experiences to produce meaning. You can then use students' prior knowledge and identified needs to design lessons about language.

Based on Van Sluys' ideas in *What If and Why? Literacy Invitations for Multilingual Classrooms* (2005), if you plan to create a unit on language that builds upon students' co-constructed ideas, then *inviting* them to participate and to share personal connections and experiences in an exploratory context is key. According to Van Sluys, invitations "state a purpose or focus for an inquiry or investigation . . . and provide or suggest tools with which to initiate and organize the activity" (2). This often takes shape on a single sheet of paper, which includes background on the invitation and topic, a list of materials to explore, and questions to consider while exploring. Van Sluys makes clear that invitations are *not* centers, and they are *not* activities that have a predetermined goal in mind. Instead, teachers design invitations with the interests of students in mind, and they craft questions to guide inquiry that students can choose to follow. Diversity in approach and perspectives is expected and encouraged, as "communicating and making meaning are group processes" (8). Van Sluys continues:

> Meaning isn't fixed; rather, it is constructed by the people interacting in particular cultural settings. We share the meaning of symbols like letters, pictures, artifacts, numbers, characters, visual images, and so forth through our interactions and shared experiences. (8)

The language invitation takes this into consideration, as it marries discussion with artifacts like photographs, newspaper clippings, video segments, and multilingual and multidialectal children's literature. These materials should be largely reflective of students' linguistic backgrounds and interests. There are three parts to the invitation: the hook, activities, and the closing.

## Your Hook: Draw Them In

Meet as a class to build excitement for language study. You may choose to watch *Yo, Yes!* (Raschka 2000) in video form (either professionally done, or of you or someone else reading the text aloud and posted to YouTube) to begin talking about language as a tool for understanding one another or read aloud a book that reflects your students' linguistic backgrounds (see **Figures 1.2** and **1.6** for suggestions). Whatever you do, make sure it grabs the attention of your students, as you will rely on their enthusiasm and engagement to carry the study forward.

## Activities: Talk About Language

Have children participate in one or more stations (see **Figure 1.2**). You may choose to continue to work as a whole class or group students to work at different stations.

| Station | Critical Questions | Possible Artifacts |
|---|---|---|
| **Photograph** | • Do you speak differently in different places? Why or why not? | Photos of<br>• playgrounds<br>• churches, mosques, synagogues<br>• variety of homes |
| **Children's Literature** | • How is each character's language like yours? How is it different? | • *Hip Hop Speaks to Children* (Giovanni 2008)<br>• *En mi familia/In My Family* (Garza 2000)<br>• *Koko's Kitten* (Patterson 1987) |
| **Advertisement** | • Is it important to be able to use language persuasively? Why or why not? | • Newspaper clippings<br>• Magazine ads |
| **Video** | • Do you ever communicate like this? When? With whom?<br>• Would you speak like this with your teacher? Why or why not? | Use a website like storylineonline.com to identify a linguistically diverse read-aloud. You can also videotape yourself reading aloud the following text(s), or find someone else reading them aloud online:<br>• *Flossie and the Fox* (McKissack 1986)<br>• *Hip Hop Speaks to Children* (Giovanni 2008)<br>• *I Love Saturdays y domingos* (Ada 2004)<br>• *My Name Is Jorge: On Both Sides of the River* (Medina 1999)<br>• *Yo, Yes!* (Raschka 2000) |

FIGURE **1.2** Language Invitation Stations

## ◻ Photograph station

Spread color and black-and-white pictures of schools, hospitals, playgrounds, grocery stores, cinemas, homes, and more around a table. As your students begin to explore, ask them some questions, such as, "How are these people speaking?" "What might they be talking about?" and "Do you speak differently in different places?" Focus them on photographs in which they are interested and ask them to consider how they think people might speak in each.

My first-grade students loved soccer, so I included images of soccer players from Mexico and the United States. Lorena and Hector had a spirited discussion about what language each group of players spoke. Lorena and Hector were from Spanish-speaking families (Guatemalan and Mexican, respectively) and lived next to one another in brightly colored trailers, from which often wafted the smells of homemade tortillas and *caldo de res* (beef soup). Both students felt comfortable using Spanish in school. Lorena once used Spanish curse words right under my nose during group-work time. I remember thinking, *Wow! She really knows how to use language to her advantage!* This conversation, then, was an important one, as it represented Lorena's and Hector's awareness of *context* when speaking. They came to consensus eventually, deciding that the Mexican flag emblazoned on one set of uniforms meant they must speak Spanish, and that the team in red, white, and blue spoke English. Lorena and Hector were thinking about language use by relying on the *place-* and *person-*based considerations people make when they use words to communicate.

In Konni Stagliano's third-grade classroom, students' home lives and beliefs came through in their ideas about the language being spoken by the people in each photograph. Their school was made up of 80 percent European American, 10 percent African American, 6 percent multiracial, and 4 percent Asian American students, and 20 percent of the children in their school were considered economically disadvantaged. On the surface, their background was quite different from the first graders I taught. I had to smile when one student looked at a photo of President Obama and stated, "He is saying taxes are going down. And he will always say what we want to hear!" I could almost picture this child sitting with her family, listening as the adults around her discussed politics while watching the news, a presidential speech, or a debate. The words sounded so adult coming from her, so steeped in rhetoric and the public's overall distrust of the government. In these ways, her language was a reflection of her family and her home life, intertwined over time and across experiences. The conversations in these classrooms are examples of how language study makes clear the interconnectedness of students' home lives and the study of words.

### ❑ Children's literature station

Display an assortment of children's literature in multiple languages and dialects across a second table. As the children explore these texts, ask them to think about the questions in **Figure 1.2**: How are these characters speaking? What are they talking about? How is each character's language like yours? How is it different? Then tailor questions to individual students as they choose books to read and discuss. In my first-grade class, many of our texts included both English and Spanish. Other texts included many families' home dialect of African American Vernacular English. Still others were in Chinese, as students expressed interest in this language during classroom discussions.

Konni's third-grade students also showed an interest in speaking and reading Spanish. "I can read Spanish!" one child excitedly told me, as he held up the bilingual book *Gathering the Sun: An Alphabet in Spanish and English* (Ada 2001). "Look!" he continued, pointing to the Spanish words on one page, "I am reading this, but I know what it says in English because it's right below it!"

### ❑ Advertisement station

Spread out a variety of newspaper clippings, magazine ads, and photos of billboards on a third table. Children may require more guidance in the advertisement station, because they may be less accustomed to examining newspaper clippings and department store printouts. Discuss the purpose of persuasive writing, which is to convince someone of something, and talk about the persuasiveness of advertising deals like two-for-one hot dogs; in these examples, authors use words to influence readers to do something. Ask students some of the following questions: "What do these ads want you to do?" "Do you ever sound like the ads do? When?" and "Is it important to be able to use language persuasively?" Consider *when* it might be important to use words persuasively. In my first-grade classroom, we also asked whether it was important to know how to speak in a variety of ways. This question came directly from previous conversations around power and how some people, like the man who called Hector's house, use words to persuade in intimidating ways.

Konni's class had studied persuasive text in the past. "Ads don't tell you the flaws," one boy pointed out, "only the good stuff. Like, you can't actually *hover* with a hover ball; you just slide—but that's not in the ad." He pointed to a photo of a bright-red sports car. "And here, you can't actually drive this car until you are sixteen, which is disappointing, but that's not in the ad, either! It just wants me to *want* the car." Many of these students, then, already understood the power of words to omit, highlight, or add information to enhance a particular point of view.

### ◻ Video station

Set up a laptop, desktop, or tablet to play a linguistically diverse children's text in video format. You can use a website like storylineonline.com to identify a linguistically diverse read-aloud. The most critical component of the video is that it demonstrates varied word use, whether in formality, dialect, or language. For the students' engagement, the video should also display the book's illustrations.

Tell each group they are going to watch a video that will display the illustrations of a book while a narrator reads the story aloud. Consider choosing one of the texts listed in the Video Station section of **Figure 1.2**; each is packed with linguistic diversity.

Ask your students to consider the way each character speaks and how it is similar to and different from the other characters. At the conclusion of the video, ask them to talk about these different ways of speaking and whether one sounds like people they know. Talk about how the students' own families, friends, and teachers use words. Do their family members like to talk on the phone? Do they talk to people at the grocery store? Do they sound the same when talking to a friend on the phone as they do when speaking to cashiers about a sale on mangos or potato chips? The questions you ask will be prompted by what you already know about your students' out-of-school experiences with language.

Konni's students watched a video read-aloud of *Yo, Yes!* (Raschka 2000) in small groups. This book, and its corresponding film, shows two young boys who use only *yo*, *yes*, and body language to communicate with one another while playing basketball. Our discussion was illuminating because we talked about students' previous understandings of how language (particularly English) changes based on whom you are speaking to.

Once the video concluded, I asked Konni's students, "Would you ever say *yo* to your teacher?"

Heads shook vigorously back and forth, and students responded by saying, "No! It's bad grammar!" or "It's slang!"

Another child said he would say *yo* to his dad, but never to a teacher, because he has a close relationship with his father. The girl next to him nodded, adding, "Yeah! Like, I use certain phrases with my family. On Sunday we dress in a 'lazy Sunday outfit.' It's like pajamas, but not pajamas. But no one here would know what I meant when I said that!"

Once again, context (based on *place* and *relationship* between speakers) was very important in the words they chose to speak to others.

## The Closing: Regroup and Summarize

After students participate in these centers, summarize and learn from one another's perspectives. Consider using a modified KWL (know; want to know; learned) chart to record what each group noticed as children gave voice to their thoughts (see **Figure 1.3**).

In my first-grade classroom, students spoke about language they used with family and language they used with friends (see **Figure 1.4**). They noticed people communicate using different languages (e.g., Chinese),

| LANGUAGE | |
|---|---|
| What did we notice? | What do we want to know? |
| | |

FIGURE **1.3**
Modified KWL Chart

FIGURE **1.4**
Modified KWL
Chart with
Student Responses

| LANGUAGE | |
|---|---|
| What did we notice? | What do we want to know? |
| • We can learn Chinese from new friends.<br>• Flossie used language to trick the fox.<br>• Language is in movies and books.<br>• Newspapers tell stories.<br>• Football and soccer use actions to tell what's happening.<br>• ZZZZ I used to show sleeping | • How can we use language to learn about each other?<br>• How and why do animals talk?<br>• How can we learn Chinese, Irish, and Spanish?<br>• Why do some English words sometimes sound different?<br>• How can we use more videos to . . . ? |

different media (newspapers, actions, movies, books), and for different purposes (to trick or persuade).

When my students discussed what they wanted to learn next about language, they wanted to know how language could help them learn about each other. They also wanted to learn about other languages (including "animal talk") and dialects ("Why do some English words sometimes sound different?"). The idea of using videos to listen to different languages and dialects interested them. They recalled the multiple languages (Spanish and English) we incorporated into a family storybook we cocreated with our loved ones and how only some families wrote their entries in Spanish (see **Figure 1.4**). The language they used varied based on the people with whom they were speaking, much like Konni's students' use of the word *yo*.

## Language Study and Formative Assessment

One challenge of language study is identifying opportunities for assessment. As you complete the language invitation and begin to consider next steps, think about students' prior knowledge of language to develop lessons that are relevant and meet the needs of your learners. Because language study stems from students' academic needs, interests, and prior knowledge, summative assessments, where a grade is assigned and students and teachers move on to new content, do not make sense. A formative assessment approach, on its own or combined with existing grammar study tests, provides teachers with documentation of student performance through a variety of collected artifacts.

You can gather data on students' use of language through artifacts such as audiotaped lessons, worksheets, observational notes, and writing samples.

Choose artifacts that are appropriate for each activity. For instance, you might want to audiotape the invitation conversation. Another useful artifact is a collection of writing samples; you might assess whether a minilesson on code switching impacted an individual's writing style, or if a student used subject-verb agreement in his or her written work after you discussed its commonality in particular contexts. Regardless of the artifacts you use, collect data throughout your language study as a way to identify students' strengths, needs, and continued interests. This will allow you to build your language study on activities that are relevant and appropriate for your students.

The Language Study Formative Assessment Guide (**Figure 1.5**) can help you focus on continuous and ongoing assessment. Use this data collection tool as you complete activities related to your language study. I recommend you use a separate guide for each student, in order to better track and analyze individual growth. The document's main body provides a space to reflect on the individual's mastery of language skills and concepts as well as areas in which growth is needed. You can also record observations about the student's interests and engagement in particular activities, along with appropriate next steps for language study. The guide's secondary table encourages you to reflect more broadly, across multiple activities. Is the student demonstrating patterns of need? Strengths? Consistent interests that might spark a long-term language study project or activity?

## How and When: Language Invitations Across Grades

Your students and their families are linguistically diverse and rich in experience. It is critical for you to envision how contextualized language study might fit into *your* classroom space, with *your* students and *your* unique pressures and time constraints. Near the end of Chapters 1 through 3, you'll find tables outlining the nitty-gritty of language study. They include descriptions of strategies and critical components organized by grade level (K–1, 2–3, and 4–6). You'll find (1) the structure of the language study component, (2) likely time allotments, and (3) classroom materials (with examples). While some aspects are the same across grade levels, pay attention to those sentences in bold, where suggestions change based on age or independence levels. Share, reorganize, slightly alter, or completely restructure these ideas—make them relevant to your students, their families, the teachers in your community, and you. See **Figure 1.6** (on page 12) for details on language invitations.

FIGURE **1.5**
Language Study
Formative Assessment
Guide

**Language Study Formative Assessment Guide**

Student Name: _____

| Language Activity/Date | Method of Data Collection (*Writing sample, worksheet, observational notes, audio recording, etc.*) | Area(s) of Strength (*Language skills/concepts in which the student shows mastery; this may be linked to grade-level standards*) | Area(s) for Growth (*Language skills/concepts in which the student did not show mastery; this may be linked to grade-level standards*) | General Observations (*Student interests, experiences, etc., as related to language study*) | Next Steps |
|---|---|---|---|---|---|
|  |  |  |  |  |  |
|  |  |  |  |  |  |
|  |  |  |  |  |  |
|  |  |  |  |  |  |

(continues)

FIGURE **1.5**
Language Study
Formative Assessment
Guide *(continued)*

As you record data from multiple activities, reflect on the following:

What patterns of language use did you identify across this student's work?

Are other students demonstrating similar needs? Does this present an opportunity for small- or whole-group lessons?

In what area(s) could this student serve as a peer model or mentor?

Based on this student's interests in language, what ideas do you have for future activities or projects?

2016 by Jen McCreight, from *Celebrating Diversity Through Language Study*. Portsmouth, NH: Heinemann.

FIGURE **1.6**
Language Invitations
Across Grades

| **Kindergarten and First Grade** |

***Structure:*** Introduction

- Open with a video or read-aloud to introduce the invitation. Discuss the purpose, station materials, and questions.

- Complete a specific invitation activity (or more than one, if you choose): photograph station, children's literature station, advertisement station, and/or video station. If you are implementing multiple activities (likely through stations), recruit an adult leader for each, to help students read the materials given and to ask them questions that focus their conversations around language.

- If other adults are present, explain the purpose of the invitation to volunteers, and share with them the importance of largely allowing the conversation among students to unfold organically. Each adult is a *guide*, asking questions to clarify and focus, but not steering the conversation toward specific answers or goals.

- *Optional Formative Assessment:* Leave an audio recorder with each group or activity to record conversations students have about language. You can listen to these recordings later to gain important knowledge about your students' understanding of words in their world. This will guide future language activities.

- Summarize with a modified KWL to learn from one another and to gather information to guide future language activities.

***Structure:*** Stations

**Photographs:**
1. How are these people speaking?
2. What might these people be talking about?
3. Do you speak differently in different places?

**Children's Literature:**
1. How are these characters speaking?
2. What are these characters talking about?
3. How is each character's language like yours? How is it different?

**Advertisements:**
1. What do these ads want you to do?
2. Do you ever sound like the ads do? When?
3. Is it important to be able to use language persuasively?

| Second and Third Grades | Fourth, Fifth, and Sixth Grades |
|---|---|
| • Open with a video or read-aloud to introduce the invitation. Discuss the purpose, station materials, and questions. | • Open with a video or read-aloud to introduce the invitation. Discuss the purpose, station materials, and questions. **Ideally, the students will be familiar with invitations; if they are not, spend time discussing the dialogic nature of invitations and the importance of hearing and learning from others.** |
| • Complete a specific activity (or more than one, if you choose): photograph station, children's literature station, advertisement station, and/or video station. **Consider your students and the activities for which they will likely need adult support in order to navigate. This will be different in different classrooms, but consider giving students full independence at the photograph station, as it is largely based on exploring pictures.** | • **Students will freely move through invitation activities, if you are implementing more than one: photograph station, children's literature station, advertisement station, and/or video station. Consider setting limits on the amount of children allowed at each station, based on the materials themselves, but encourage students to examine language from the point of view that most interests them.** |
| • If other adults are present, explain the purpose of the invitation to volunteers, and share with them the importance of largely allowing the conversation among students to unfold organically. Each adult is a *guide*, asking questions to clarify and focus, but not steering the conversation toward specific answers or goals. | • **Teachers and adult leaders listen to students and ask questions or offer help as needed, but only to guide the conversation, not to steer students toward predetermined responses.** |
| • *Optional Formative Assessment:* Leave an audio recorder with each group or activity to record conversations students have about language. You can listen to these recordings later to gain important knowledge about your students' understanding of words in their world. This will guide future language activities. | • *Optional Formative Assessment:* Leave an audio recorder with each group or activity to record conversations students have about language. You can listen to these recordings later to gain important knowledge about your students' understanding of words in their world. This will guide future language activities. |
| • Summarize with a modified KWL to learn from one another and to gather information to guide future language activities. | • Summarize with a modified KWL to learn from one another and to gather information to guide future language activities. |
| **Photographs:**<br>1. How are these people speaking?<br>2. What might these people be talking about?<br>3. Do you speak differently in different places? | **Photographs:**<br>1. How are these people speaking?<br>2. What might these people be talking about?<br>3. Do you speak differently in different places?<br>4. **How do you think the language people use changes, based on where they are?** |
| **Children's Literature:**<br>1. How are these characters speaking?<br>2. What are these characters talking about?<br>3. How is each character's language like yours? How is it different? | **Children's Literature:**<br>1. How are these characters speaking?<br>2. What are these characters talking about?<br>3. How is each character's language like yours? How is it different?<br>4. **Whose language is *not* usually represented in these places? How do you feel about this?** |
| **Advertisements:**<br>1. What do these ads want you to do?<br>2. Do you ever sound like the ads do? When?<br>3. **What kinds of words do the advertisements use so people will buy certain things?**<br>4. Is it important to be able to use language persuasively? | **Advertisements:**<br>1. What do these ads want you to do?<br>2. Do you ever sound like the ads do? When?<br>3. **What kinds of words do the advertisements use so people will buy certain things?**<br>4. Is it important to be able to use language persuasively? |

*(continues)*

FIGURE **1.6**
Language Invitations
Across Grades
*(continued)*

## Kindergarten and First Grade

*Structure:* Stations
*(continued)*

**Videos:**
1. How did these characters communicate?
2. Do you ever communicate like this? When? With whom?
3. Would you speak like this to your teacher? Why or why not?

## Kindergarten Through Sixth Grade

*Time Allotment:* Approximately ten to twenty minutes per station or activity

*Materials:* Stations

**Language Invitation Introduction:**
1. Read-aloud
2. Written invitation to students to study language
   (see "Materials: Invitation to Students" section)
3. Short opening video, like *Yo, Yes!* (Raschka 2000)
4. Audio recorder (optional)

**Photograph Station:**
1. Forty to fifty photographs of familiar places (playgrounds; schools; churches, mosques, synagogues; homes; restaurants)
2. Question sheet (see the "Structure: Stations" section of table)
3. Audio recorder (optional)

**Children's Literature Station:**
1. Ten to fifteen picture books written in a variety of languages and dialects (see "Materials: Literature" section)
2. Question sheet (see "Structure: Station Questions" section)
3. Audio recorder (optional)

**Advertisement Station:**
1. Forty to fifty newspaper clippings and magazine ads of familiar products (food, toys, games, clothing)
2. Question sheet (see "Structure: Stations" section)
3. Audio recorder (optional)

**Video Station:**
1. Laptop or iPad (with video open and ready to play)
2. Short (ten-minute) video of a read-aloud of a linguistically diverse children's book (see examples on page 4)
3. Question sheet (see "Structure: Stations" section)
4. Audio recorder (optional)

**Conclusion:**
1. Modified KWL chart (see **Figure 1.3**)
2. Audio recorder (optional)

**Videos:**
1. How did these characters communicate?
2. Do you ever communicate like this? When? With whom?
3. Would you speak like this to your teacher? Why or why not?

**Videos:**
1. How did these characters communicate?
2. Do you ever communicate like this? When? With whom?
3. Would you speak like this to your teacher? Why or why not?

**Materials:** Literature

The following examples are appropriate across grade levels, both with (in younger grades) and without (in older grades) an adult reader present. I recommend using picture books no matter the grade level, as the complexity in and length of chapter books make it more difficult to consider linguistic diversity. These books are a representative sample of linguistically diverse texts highlighting African American Vernacular English and Spanish, but you could include literature in other languages and dialects as well.

**African American Vernacular English:**

Giovanni, Nikki. 2008. *Hip Hop Speaks to Children: A Celebration of Poetry with a Beat*. Naperville, IL: Sourcebooks.

Greenfield, Eloise. 1974. *She Come Bringin' Me That Little Baby Girl*. New York: HarperCollins.

———. 1978. *Honey, I Love, and Other Poems*. New York: HarperCollins Children's Books.

hooks, bell. 1999. *Happy to Be Nappy*. New York: Jump at the Sun.

McKissack, Patricia. 1986. *Flossie and the Fox*. New York: Dial Books.

Williams, Sherley. A. 1997. *Working Cotton*. Orlando, FL: Harcourt Brace.

**Spanish:**

Ada, Alma. F. 2004. *I love Saturdays y domingos*. New York: Atheneum Books.

Alarcon, Francisco. X. 1997. *Jitomates risuenos: Y otros poemas de primavera/Laughing Tomatoes: And Other Spring Poems*. San Francisco: Children's Book Press.

———. 1998. *Del ombligo de la luna: Y otros poemas de verano/From the Bellybutton of the Moon: And Other Summer Poems*. San Francisco: Children's Book Press.

———. 2001. *Iguanas an la nieve: Y otros poemas de invierno/Iguanas in the Snow: And Other Winter Poems*. San Francisco: Children's Book Press.

———. 2005. *Los angeles andan en bicicleta: Y otros poemas do otoño/Angels Ride Bikes: And Other Fall Poems*. San Francisco: Children's Book Press.

Cisneros, Sandra. 1997. *Hairs/Pelitos: A Story in English and Spanish*. New York: Dragonfly Books.

Garza, Carmen. L. 1993. *Cuadros de familia/Family Pictures*. San Francisco: Children's Book Press.

———. 2000. *En mi familia/In My Family*. San Francisco: Children's Book Press.

Medina, Jane. 1999. *My Name Is Jorge: On Both Sides of the River*. Honesdale, PA: Boyds Mills Press.

Perez, Amada. I. 2009. *Mi diario de aqui hasta alla/My Diary from Here to There*. San Francisco: Children's Book Press.

**Materials:** Invitation to Students

The following text could be typed or written on chart paper.

> *Dear Class,*
>
> *We use language every day. We use it in our homes, our schools, and our community. It is part of everything we do, so I am inviting you to study language with me. We will be explorers and detectives, finding words in the world and thinking about how we use them.*
>
> *Let's start today. We will look at books, newspapers and magazines, and photographs. We will even watch a video! I invite you to think about how words are being used at each station. Then, we'll share as a whole class.*
>
> *I hope you accept my invitation!*
>
> *Sincerely,*
>
> *Your Teacher*

# Opportunities for Family–School Partnerships

Integrating family perspectives into language study is not just something we *should* do but something we *can* do. One way to get started is with family dialogue journals.

Family dialogue journals (FDJs) contain journal entries written from student to family member(s) and back again. These entries are always an extension of a school topic, with the student opening up dialogue by sharing what she or he has learned in school and asking family members a question related to that topic. Family members then respond to the question, in their home language and in their own way, and students share these responses with the class. Students and teachers learn about the rich diversity present within their community, which opens up opportunities for future conversation. Teachers can respond to the entries, connecting their own experiences or asking questions for further discussion. Create a schedule that works for you and your students. It is important to note that FDJs are not behavior based and are never used to record notes about a student's "bad day." They are also not punitive, and their completion should never factor into a child's grade. Finally, be sure to identify options for translating FDJ entries into students' home languages, as my coteacher, Walter Avila, did every week for us (Walter is originally from Honduras). In order for meaningful dialogue around classroom topics to occur, this written space must be safe and accessible for all involved (Allen et al. 2015).

There are many ways to use FDJs in your classroom—writing a co-constructed class letter, splitting up into groups to tackle different topics, allowing each student to choose his or her own topic or question (Allen et al. 2015). My students and I decided on a topic each week after voting on choices in a compiled list. Then we made a web of words we might need to know how to spell and constructed a class letter to practice and think through our ideas (see **Figures 1.7** and **1.8**).

Then, think through challenges you might face. How will you translate journal entries for families who speak different languages at home? How will you respond if

Since language study is not a common approach to studying grammar and words in the world, you may want to send a letter to families that explains the work you will be doing. Here is an example letter:

Dear family,

This year, your child will be engaging in language study. Instead of studying only the rules of grammar and insisting on one way of speaking all the time, we will be thinking about how we speak and write based on context (who we are speaking to, and where we are). We will also learn about different ways of speaking and writing by building on the words and phrases we already use to communicate with family, friends, and other grown-ups or acquaintances.

We would love you to be a part of our work. We invite you to share your perspective on the way you use words in your world (at home, at work, etc.). We will be sending home journals, questionnaires, invitations to our classroom, and more—but, please know we would love to learn from you at any time!

Let me know if you have any questions. I look forward to speaking with you soon.

Sincerely,

students consistently bring back blank journal response pages—or nothing at all?

Many teachers have dealt with these (and other) questions and uncertainties around FDJs. If you are interested in learning more about how a variety of teachers from grades K through 12 implemented FDJs in their classrooms, and how they navigated these challenges, see *Family Dialogue Journals: School–Home Partnerships That Support Student Learning* (Allen et al. 2015).

Would you consider using family dialogue journals in your classroom? If so, take some time to imagine what this might look like. How will you structure journal time? What types of journals will you use—composition books, three-ring binders, or spiral-bound books? How often will students write in the journals, and how much time will students and families have to return them?

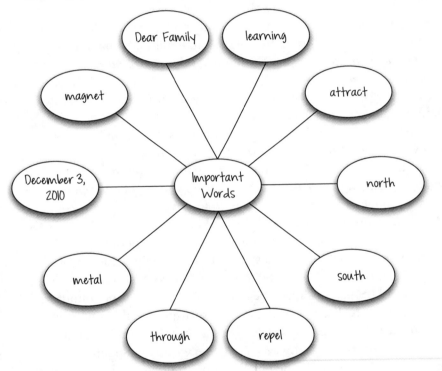

FIGURE **1.7**
Web of Important Words

FIGURE **1.8**
Example Class Letter

We also constructed a class question for families, considering whether it would lead to a detailed response. All students wrote their own journal entries to families, either using the supportive class letter or constructing their own.

With my first graders, the link between FDJs and language

Dear <u>family</u>

We are Learning about magnets.

They attract to metal.

Where have you seen magnets in the world?

Love,

emerged quite naturally. They were already code switching and considering their audience while writing, which meant they were ready for more intentional discussion around when such code switching is necessary.

The connection emerged when we wrote to families about our "first-grade hopes and dreams." After finishing our co-constructed letter, I handed out brand-new black-and-white composition notebooks for the children to write to their families. The newness of the journals, the possibility inherent in their blank pages, seemed to fuel the children, and soon they were seated at desks, on pillows, or under tables with friends, guiding their pencils carefully and deliberately across the first white page.

I rotated around the room, conferring with students as needed, pausing only to write in each journal the question to families: "What are your hopes and dreams for me this year?" I stopped to write "*¿Cual es son sus suenos y esperanzas para mi?*" in Naldo's journal, as his family primarily spoke Spanish, and my coteacher had already translated our focal question into this common familial home language.

I glanced at Naldo's writing, which already consisted of multiple sentences. My eyes widened when I realized he was writing his entry entirely in Spanish! He was a fearless speller, stretching out the sounds he heard and proudly displaying *keyro* as his sound-spelled version of *quiero*; he wrote that his hope for the year was to learn to drive a car.

"My mom wants me to learn Spanish and English this year. She will teach me to read in Spanish and I will teach her English, because she doesn't know much English yet and she wants me to help her learn," Naldo shared with me as I took in his biliterate writing. As Naldo turned his face back toward his paper, already beginning to stretch out the sounds in his next sentence, I realized I was the one most surprised and impressed by his linguistic risk taking. For Naldo, it was a natural extension of his growing mastery of sounds. Why *wouldn't* he be writing in Spanish, since his family speaks Spanish at home and this journal was meant to be shared with his family?

Naldo was already aware of the fact that he needed to contextualize the way he used language. He had never attempted to write to *me* in Spanish, because he knew I was not a fluent Spanish speaker; while writing to his mother, however, he found Spanish to be the most appropriate form of communication. Naldo was able to tell me about his plans to teach his mother English and to learn how to write in Spanish from her, further illustrating his willingness to broaden his use of language (both written and spoken).

# 2

# CREATING TRANSLATION CHARTS |

## "That's Not *My* Book Talk!"

One morning, I sat at a table with Hector, Jorge, and Elijah during writing workshop. Elijah and Hector were writing independently, concentrating on creating informational texts about space and Pokémon. I was reading and writing with Jorge as he composed a book about dogs.

He giggled as he wrote the following: "Dog can be running."

I repeated the words exactly as he had written them on his paper. Without any prompting, Jorge then said back, "It should be *dogs* for books."

Looking up from his book, Hector chimed in, "Jorge's book was *friend* talk."

"That's not *my* book talk," Elijah then countered. "I would say, 'Dogs *are* running.'"

"*Los perros corren,*" Hector chimed in, proudly demonstrating for us the Spanish translation of Jorge's sentence with a big smile on his face. "That's my language," Hector said proudly.

## Translation Charts

Spanish was Hector's language, a language in which he demonstrated considerable expertise and knowledge. It was important to recognize his expertise as such because, as Rymes stated,

> without being recognized as competent speakers of the language they learned before school, students may not be able to make connections between the depth of their childhood language socialization and the new language they are learning in the classroom. Drawing connections between the two provides openings for deeper learning in the classroom. (2009, 41)

The conversation between Hector, Elijah, and Jorge came about after our class created translation charts. By creating translation charts, the next building block in a language study, you will engage students through a linguistically diverse mentor text and allow them to experiment with language. Students translate words and phrases they say in particular contexts (say, with family) into how they would convey the same messages in different contexts (e.g., with a teacher at school). This activity builds on the work of teachers in Shirley Brice Heath's *Ways with Words* ([1983] 1996) as well as Wheeler and Swords' (2004) research. In Heath's long-term ethnographic study with multiple communities of diverse language learners, she observed teachers using a similar activity. Specifically, teachers' goals were

1. to provide a foundation of familiar knowledge to serve as context for classroom information;
2. to engage students in collecting and analyzing familiar ways of knowing and translating these into . . . school-accepted labels, concepts, and generalizations; and
3. to provide students with meaningful opportunities to learn ways of talking about using language to organize and express information. ([1983] 1996, 340)

Years later, Swords, a primary-grade classroom teacher, worked with Wheeler to redevelop her language curriculum by building on the perspectives and needs of her students. After discussing how people change their clothing based on where they are going (you would not wear the same clothing at a wedding as you might wear to play basketball, the students agreed), Swords and her students created a language-focused T-chart. They labeled one side "Formal" (standardized English) and the other side "Informal" (AAVE). Using examples from her students' written work and contrasting them with phrases the students often used when speaking, Swords and the children sorted sentences into two categories. Swords found that her students "were able to use their own prior knowledge to define formal and informal language" (Wheeler and Swords 2004, 475) without the commonly used drill and practice of pulling apart isolated sentences.

The translation charts my students and I used were similar. However, we thought it was just as important to consider the relationships between speakers in a conversation as it was to consider the place where the conversation occurred. Many students in my school spoke to their teachers using standardized English (SE), but I often watched these same students fly by me on the playground, calling out to one another, "You best be runnin' faster!"

School was the *place* for each of these exchanges, and yet it was the *relationship* between speakers that most affected the words they chose. The translation charts I describe here are at once focused on place *and* relationship. You will build upon your students' interests and background knowledge while scaffolding them to think more about the effect context has on the words and phrases they use.

Translation charts are tools to help your students discuss the choices they make in language. Consider Hector switching from English to Spanish when he spoke about the cats living at his home to Walter Avila and me. He did not pause between sentences, thinking about what he was going to say; instead, he seamlessly moved from one language to another, saying, "I have kittens. There is a black one and a white one. No, *el gato no tiene nombre.*" He did what any of us would if speaking to friends versus our boss or coworkers versus a waitress at our favorite restaurant. Hector was ready to use his own experiences with language to think about code switching and language rules. And based on Mack's discussion with Ruby about the relationship between skin color and language, and Lorena's debate over the languages spoken by national soccer teams, I believed many other students were as ready as Hector. Translation charts help us categorize shifts in word use while still recognizing the importance of individual students' backgrounds and experiences. They helped us create a common metalanguage to discuss linguistic diversity.

## Your Hook: Introduce Translation Charts

Pull up the modified KWL you completed as a summarizing activity, and build your conversation from these written words. What do students remember about how they use words? What were some things they wanted to learn about language?

Provide younger students with a visual that connects language study, which is rather abstract, to something more concrete. Wheeler and Swords (2004) helped students think about language categories by talking about categories of clothing, which can be both effective and fun! Pull out articles of clothing like a bathrobe, winter outerwear, and a feather boa, and ask your students some questions about where these items are usually worn. Would they wear the bathrobe to school? The coat to the beach in the summer? The feather boa to the grocery store? Use this to teach them that just as they change the clothing they wear based on where they are going and what they are doing, so does language.

Begin to analyze language through the use of a linguistically diverse text, one that uses multiple languages or dialects or that clearly shows characters engaged in both formal and informal conversation (see **Figure 2.6** for text suggestions). Tell students they will be thinking about how characters speak in different ways, and ask students to listen for these differences as you read. It is important to use a text that you have previously read aloud, since the students should already understand the plot and be familiar with the characters; this will help them to focus on the language each character is using this time. What differences do students hear between characters as they speak? Ask questions like one of the following:

- Does this character sound like you do when you speak to your family? Your friends? Why or why not?
- How does [character] sound the same as [another character]? How do they sound different from each other?

My first graders and I read the folktale *Flossie and the Fox* (McKissack 1986). It features the AAVE-speaking Flossie and the SE-speaking fox and plays on the oft-portrayed relationship between young girls and cunning, humanlike animals. However, instead of being easily influenced, Flossie does not bow down to the cunning fox. When he tries to steal her basket of eggs, Flossie convinces the fox he must prove he is a fox for her to be appropriately scared. In the end, Flossie outsmarts him, sending the fox running from hound dogs while still trying to prove his identity. I chose this book because of my students' familiarity with and love of it, as well as its incorporation of two dialects commonly represented in our classroom. The characters' distinct ways of speaking provided multiple opportunities for us to compare their use of language with our own.

In Konni Stagliano's third-grade class, we read *I Love Saturdays y domingos* (Ada 2004). This text is narrated from the perspective of a young girl whose grandparents on one side of the family speak English and grandparents on the other side speak Spanish. She loves spending time with them both, and the text describes what she does with each set of grandparents. On *domingo*, Spanish for *Sunday*, the girl code switches between English and Spanish as she recounts her day with *abuelito y abuelita*, giving readers who do not speak Spanish the chance to learn words and phrases. We chose this book because of the students' interest in the Spanish texts they explored during our language invitation.

You can introduce the term *code switching*, as you will discuss this concept throughout a language study. Explain to students that we code switch when we change the way we talk from place to place or from person to person (Nilep 2006). Students may recognize they speak differently to their teachers in class than they do to their friends while on the playground. We all code switch, and by defining and using this term with children, you will help them to verbalize their own experiences with code switching.

As my students and I read *Flossie and the Fox*, they offered comments about the characters' use of language. Early in our conversation, Michael stated that the fox spoke "proper" and like he was in a ceremony or a courtroom. This reflected Michael's penchant for courtroom dramas, which his mom said he often snuck glimpses of while perusing YouTube. Wanting to build on this as I read the book, I asked the students if they could give me an example of words in their world that were similar to the "proper," ceremonious way the fox spoke. Daisy immediately raised her hand, and said, "The fox be like Barack Obama when he talking."

"Do you think Barack Obama speaks the same at home with his kids and wife as he does when he is on stage giving a speech?" I asked. I knew the students were familiar with Obama as a formal speaker, since we had communally listened to his address for students earlier in the year. We had even written him letters, and many of the students had commented on his knack for giving speeches. One student had written, "Dear President Obama, I love your speaking. Is the speaking fun? I like how you speak" (see **Figure 2.1**).

The children smiled at the thought of Obama speaking so formally to his family. "He don't use speech talk," Dahlia offered, shaking her head from left to right. The other students agreed, smiling as they considered that even President Obama needed to reflect on whom he was talking to when moving from place to place and from person to person.

FIGURE **2.1**
Student Letter to Barack Obama

When I asked Konni's students why they thought the young girl in *I Love Saturdays y domingos* was speaking in two different languages with her grandparents, one child stated, "Because one speaks English and the other Spanish; you speak to them so they can understand."

"Oh," I said, "so you can change how you talk to people so they understand you?" Already, these third graders were considering the importance of shifting how we speak based on context.

These early conversations, pulling in language from our mentor texts, allowed us to communally construct our understanding of how people spoke in different situations.

Dear President Obama,

I Love your specing.

Is the specing fun?

I like how you spec.

# Activity: Create a Translation Chart

After reading a mentor text and thinking carefully about the languages the characters are using, begin a translation chart. The main purpose of the translation chart is to consider how the language you use shifts based on the person with whom you are speaking. This, then, will influence students' ability to determine which social situations call for the use of particular codes (such as standardized English). Creating translation charts will remind them that a variety of codes are valid and valuable and that particular situations will call for the use of particular codes; the more options they have in their linguistic toolbox (Wheeler and Swords 2004), the better able they will be to successfully navigate a variety of conversations and writing assignments.

Pull out chart paper, and tell your students to discuss how they use language with different people and in different places, just like the characters in their book. We charted the language we used with three different groups of people: family, friends, and other grown-ups (see **Figure 2.2** for the blank chart). These were three important relationships for my students, as they spent a majority of their time with family and friends, but they also spoke regularly to teachers, student teachers, principals, and university visitors.

You might categorize your chart in other ways, based on what you learned about your students' language use during the language invitation. Whatever the categories are, personalizing them based on your students' interests and backgrounds will help you see the nuances present in everyday language use. Even more, you and your students will realize how you "learn words from particular people in particular interactive events" (Dyson 2001a, 419) and how you are likely to use similar words and sentence structures with comparable people in the future. Hector knew this when he moved from English to Spanish while talking about his animals with Walter and me; his relationship with each of us, and what he knew about the language we used, governed the construction of his response.

FIGURE **2.2**
Blank Translation Chart

| Language: How Do I Use It? | | |
|---|---|---|
| With Family | With Friends | With Other Grown-Ups |
| | | |

Begin your discussion by referring to the language of the characters in your book. Ask the children questions like, "Which characters spoke most like your friends?" "Who spoke most like your family?" "Who sounds like your teachers or principal?" and "Why do you think this?" This will help the children transition between discussing the language of *characters* and discussing the language of *familiar people*. My first graders unanimously identified Flossie's speech as being most similar to their peers and family, while the fox sounded like other grown-ups they knew.

Next, have students translate, or code switch, words and phrases within the multiple categories on your chart. Let them know they should think about how their words change within each category, even though the message they are conveying stays the same. I usually start by translating greetings, because greetings are something we all use, and we do so with people in many different contexts. Ask your students: "How do you greet your family when you wake up in the morning? How do you greet your friends when you see them at school? How do you greet grown-ups in the hallway as you walk to your classroom?" With younger students, you may do this as a whole class; as students respond, record their ideas on the translation chart. With older students ready for more independence, you may place students in groups or partnerships to translate greetings. Hand out sticky notes so they can record their ideas and then stick each contribution to a larger translation chart.

> What are some other ideas for an opening translation chart lesson? What are some other situations and contexts where your students speak with many different people?

### ◻ First grade

My first graders had a variety of responses (see **Figure 2.3**). They identified formal speech ("Welcome to you") with sentiment they might share with grown-ups they did not know very well. Their links to *family* talk included phrases in both English and Spanish, which reflected the fact that

FIGURE **2.3**
Completed First-Grade Translation Chart

| Language: How Do I Use It? | | |
|---|---|---|
| With Family | With Friends | With Other Grown-Ups |
| "Hello."<br>"Hola."<br>"Whatcha doin?"<br>"Hola. ¿Como estas?" | "Hey, what's up?"<br>"Hello, friend."<br>"Sup dude!"<br>"Sup old man." | "Welcome to you." |

many of them spoke Spanish at home. Their examples of *friend* talk were wide-ranging, including the more common "Hey, what's up?" and the more obscure "Sup, old man."

Jacob's example of "Sup, old man," which he interjected immediately following Hector's "Sup, dude," was met with large smiles. Fits of giggles ensued when I asked him how this response would differ if he were greeting his principal, and he responded, "Sup, old lady!" The humor was almost lost on me, as I began to worry that our principal would somehow unluckily choose that moment to pop her head into our room to say hello. I wanted the children to play with language as they considered the nuanced differences between greetings, but maybe this was too much.

Upon reflection, however, I realized that Jacob's and his classmates' giggles at this suggestion showed their awareness that this greeting might not be well received by our principal (or any other adults, for that matter). And hadn't I hoped for exactly this sort of realization in creating this lesson? Jacob's use of language deliberately, and somewhat forcefully, toppled traditional rules regulating the exchange of words between authority figures and subordinates; at the same time, he was aware of his current audience. While he (probably) would not have said "Sup, old lady!" to our principal, he knew his friends would find this use of language funny, and for this response, he pushed his linguistic limits within the safety of our classroom space. This boundary pushing helped us to think about not only what *was* considered common language in particular contexts but also what *was not*.

### ◻ Third grade

In Konni's room, we began by modeling for the children what it looked like to translate greetings into *friend, family,* and *other grown-up* talk. Then we divided the children into groups of four, assigning one child in each group the task of recording responses onto sticky notes. The sticky notes were color coded to make it easier for students to remember the three ways they were translating greetings. Pink represented family, orange represented friends, and blue represented other grown-ups. After the students had worked in groups to discuss how they would greet people in each of these contexts, they placed sticky notes on the chart (see **Figure 2.4**).

Immediately, patterns emerged, even though the children had not been working together as a whole class. This is the advantage of breaking into groups; more students have the opportunity to contribute to the chart, and as a class you can sort the notes based on patterns you are seeing across

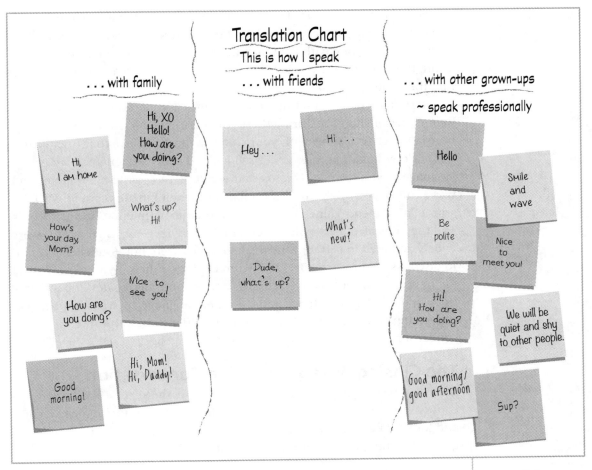

FIGURE **2.4**
Completed Third-Grade
Translation Chart

groups. For instance, "Good morning," "What's up?" and "Hi" were included multiple times in both the "With Friends" and the "With Family" categories. However, "What's up?" and "Hi" were included much less frequently
in the "With Other Grown-Ups" section. Instead, phrases like "Nice to meet
you" featured more prominently. In addition, some groups included descriptions of their demeanor when speaking with a less familiar grown-up. They
noted they would be shy and that it was important to speak politely. When
we discussed this as a class, many children said these differences were because you "speak professionally" with adults you do not know very well.

Interestingly, much like Jacob did in my first-grade classroom, one
student pushed typical linguistic boundaries when he encouraged his
group to add "Sup?" to the "With Other Grown-Ups" column. When other

students saw this, some exclaimed, "You wouldn't say that to someone you didn't know!" Others giggled, and the child who suggested the sticky note beamed, happy with the reaction he was getting from his peers. Once again, this student was playing with language, and our chart work gave him the opportunity to do so.

Both first graders and third graders found it important to push the boundaries of language during these conversations. As you engage in translation chart lessons with your students, push against your own inclinations of what is appropriate for school, and allow students to play with language as you study it. I was certainly not perfect in these moments, and was at times downright uncomfortable, but when I made room for such wordplay, students gained confidence in their experimentation with words, and they revealed a great deal about their knowledge of which words were widely accepted in certain contexts and which were not. Students began to discuss sentence structures and word choice on their own. They allowed me to be part of these conversations, as they continued to develop a shared understanding of how they could shift their language choices to fit particular contexts. Translation chart lessons were the start of this intentional conversation around how we contextualize language.

## The Closing: Wrap Up with a Conversation

After you record students' responses about how they speak in different contexts, you will be ready to close your lesson. This is a time for reflection and for sharing what you and the students noticed about their use of language. You might ask questions like the following:

- Based on our discussion, do you greet people the same, no matter who they are?
- Why might you greet one person differently than another?
- Are there other times, besides when saying hello, when we change the way we speak based on where we are or based on whom we are speaking to?
- How can you use what we learned about different ways of speaking when you are reading and writing? When might you use *friend* or *family* talk in your writing? When might you use *other grown-up* talk? Why?

As you discuss students' answers, continue to pay attention to what they find interesting about language. Also take note of what you are learning about their language backgrounds. Write these observations (from general discussion, an audiotaped recording of your conversations, or what you wrote on the translation chart) on your Language Study Formative Assessment Guide (see **Figure 1.5**). Continue to analyze students' linguistic challenges and strengths by studying these artifacts.

Wrap up your translation chart activity by posting the chart in a prominent place and offering to continue the conversation. For instance, you can encourage the children to report to you or independently write down other interesting examples of how they greet different people in their lives, based on relationship and context. Or you can post a blank translation chart next to the one you completed and use teachable moments throughout your day or week to record examples of language that would likely change based on context. For instance, if you hear a student say, "Whoa, dude!" in praise of a friend's completed art project, decide as a class which category this phrase would fit into on your chart. Discuss how this phrase would shift if the student were speaking to someone who represented another of your identified categories of language use.

## Extension Activity: Standards-Based Translation Charts

Up until this point, the language invitation and translation charts have largely been based on students' own lives and experiences. Recognizing the validity of students' home languages and dialects is critical to developing relevance in language study; recognizing the fact that societal and school standards will likely ask them to communicate using standardized English is critical to the practical nature of this work.

As a next step you might create a translation chart that contextualizes words and phrases spoken by others while still using categories your students created. First, identify (through either observation, a test, or their writing) a grade-level standard in English language arts, likely related to speaking or writing standardized English, that your students are not yet contextualizing. Instead, they are speaking or writing using their home language or dialect, without effectively considering their audience or the purpose of their communication. Again, it's important to note they are not using language incorrectly, but differently than what the context of school is asking them to do. For instance, I often observed students replacing *is* with the word *be* in sentences like "She be comin' down the hall." This led me to the assumption that they had not yet practiced code switching their subject-verb agreement to reflect standardized English. So I knew I would base my new translation chart on this standard.

Then, think of a sentence in this area that your students would likely say belongs in their *family* or *friend* category but that would shift within the context of school. It may be something you've heard them say on the playground or in the lunchroom, or you may pull dialogue from a character in a familiar text. Next, create a new chart, with your students' categories heading the sections. Write your sentence in the appropriate category before presenting the chart to your students. With my first graders, I borrowed a sentence spoken by Flossie in *Flossie and the Fox* (McKissack 1986): "'Ms. Viola's chickens be so scared!' said Flossie." I placed it in the "With Family" column because the children said Flossie spoke like their family and friends, while her nemesis, the fox, spoke like other grown-ups. I chose this particular sentence because it reflected an opportunity to shift from AAVE to SE, as our grade-level standard was asking us to do.

Once you choose a standard and a sentence, show the new translation chart to your students. This might be during morning meeting, as a warm-up grammar exercise, or when you have five minutes left before heading to lunch. After reading the sentence aloud, ask them: "Why is the sentence in this particular category? Where or with whom have you heard it?" and, more specifically, "Are there words or phrases in the sentence that make you think it should stay in this category?" Finally, ask, "What word(s) could you change to shift the sentence to another category?"

When my students and I engaged in this activity, we had never discussed subject-verb agreement. And yet, when I asked them to change one word in that *family* talk sentence to make it sound more like a sentence spoken by other grown-ups, there was no hesitation in their response. Quickly and decisively, they raised their hands and whispered to each other, with some saying, "Change *be*!" Lorena said, "Change *be*, and make it say *are*." I wrote the sentence with this change in the "With Other Grown-Ups" column, drawing boxes around *be* and *are* to highlight the change (see **Figure 2.5**).

FIGURE **2.5**
*Flossie and the Fox*
Translation Chart

| Language: How Do I Use It? | | |
| --- | --- | --- |
| With Family | With Friends | With Other Grown-Ups |
| "Ms. Viola's chickens be so scared!" said Flossie. | | Ms. Viola's chickens are so scared!" said Flossie. " |

My students demonstrated their ability to apply their growing understanding of how language changes based on context in order to create a sentence spoken by other grown-ups (which they associated with SE). They showed they could incorporate subject-verb agreement into their speech and writing. I would simply need to refer to our cocreated categories to cue them to make these shifts!

Even more, their eagerness to engage in code switching made clear they found multiple ways of speaking valid and relevant. They knew how to create sentences with subject-verb agreement (the standard I initially believed they had not yet mastered) when it was contextualized within the categories of language use they had created. Within this space, translation was seemingly effortless, as evidenced by the speed and accuracy of their responses.

When you initially ask your own students to move beyond their lived experiences to translate sentences that are spoken by others, I encourage you to pay close attention to what they know. While they may not be familiar with particular vocabulary or terminology related to the standard you chose (*subject-verb agreement*, for instance), they might be able to use the categories you cocreated to demonstrate their ability to implement the rule behind the standard itself. From here, you can teach them the academic language, or vocabulary, all in the context of categories they have explored and cocreated.

## How and When: Translation Charts Across Grades

In **Figure 2.6**, you will find additional guidance on creating translation chart lessons. (See p. 9 for more information if you skipped the first chapter.) Remember that sentences in bold indicate changes I suggest based on age or independence levels. Modify these ideas in any way you see fit.

FIGURE **2.6**
Translation Charts
Across Grades

| **Kindergarten and First Grade** |
| --- |

***Structure:*** Translation Charts

- Open by displaying the completed KWL chart and discussing what you remember about your language invitation.

- Engage your students by wearing various pieces of out-of-place clothing, and discuss the context in which you would wear each one. Link this to the importance of context in the words you choose.

- Read a children's picture book that includes dialogue or text in multiple languages or dialects. As you read, ask questions about how the author and particular characters are using language in different ways. Who sounds like the children's family or friends? Who speaks differently? Where have they heard someone sound like [character]?

- Display a blank translation chart with the categories you have predetermined, and tell the students you will be recording phrases and sentences they have heard in each category. Then they will translate each as it would change based on context.

- Ask the children to give examples of how they would greet someone according to one of your predetermined categories (e.g., friends, family, etc.). Then translate these greetings into another category.

- Close by asking what the students noticed about how they use words.

- Post your completed translation chart. Add to it when students hear or think of other examples of greetings. Or post a blank translation chart to record and translate sentences students are interested in throughout the week.

| Second and Third Grades | Fourth, Fifth, and Sixth Grades |
|---|---|
| • Open by displaying the completed KWL chart and discussing what you remember about your language invitation. | • Open by displaying the completed KWL chart and discussing what you remember about your language invitation. |
| • Engage your students by wearing various pieces of out-of-place clothing, and discuss the context in which you would wear each one. Link this to the importance of context in the words you choose. | • **The clothing analogy may not be as effective for older students, so you may decide to skip this activity.** |
| • Read a children's picture book that includes dialogue or text in multiple languages or dialects. As you read, ask questions about how the author and particular characters are using language in different ways. Who sounds like the children's family or friends? Who speaks differently? Where have they heard someone sound like [character]? | • Read a children's picture book that includes dialogue or text in multiple languages or dialects. As you read, ask questions about how the author and particular characters are using language in different ways. Who sounds like the children's family or friends? Who speaks differently? Where have they heard someone sound like [character]? |
| • Display a blank translation chart with the categories you have predetermined, and tell the students you will be recording phrases and sentences they have heard in each category. Then they will translate each as it would change based on context. | • Display a blank translation chart with the categories you have predetermined, and tell the students you will be recording phrases and sentences they have heard in each category. Then they will translate each as it would change based on context. |
| • Ask the children to give examples of how they would greet someone according to one of your predetermined categories (e.g., friends, family, etc.). Then translate these greetings into another category. **Consider dividing students into small groups, with each group translating greetings in each category on sticky notes. Then display them all on one chart and share group responses as a class.** | • Ask the children to give examples of how they would greet someone according to one of your predetermined categories (e.g., friends, family, etc.). Then translate these greetings into another category.<br>• **Consider dividing students into small groups, with each group translating greetings in each category on sticky notes. Then display them all on one chart and share group responses as a class.**<br>• **Each time the children translate, ask them *why* this switch happens, leading them to think about how relationships and formality affect how they speak to others.** |
| • Close by asking what the students noticed about how they use words. **Which of these ways of speaking and writing would they use in a letter to the president? To their best friend? To their uncle who sent them a birthday gift? Why?**<br>• **Which would they likely use when completing an assignment for school? Why?** | • Close by asking what the students noticed about how they use words. **Which of these ways of speaking and writing would they use in a letter to the president? To their best friend? To their uncle who sent them a birthday gift? Why?**<br>• **Which would they likely use when completing an assignment for school? Why?** |
| • Post your completed translation chart. Add to it when students hear or think of other examples of greetings. Or post a blank translation chart to record and translate sentences students are interested in throughout the week. | • Post your completed translation chart. Add to it when students hear or think of other examples of greetings. Or post a blank translation chart to record and translate sentences students are interested in throughout the week. |

*(continues)*

FIGURE **2.6**
Translation Charts
Across Grades
(*continued*)

## Kindergarten Through Sixth Grade

***Time Allotment:*** Fifty minutes to one hour

- Hook: twenty to twenty-five minutes
- Creating the chart: twenty to twenty-five minutes
- Closing: ten minutes

### *Materials:*

*Hook:*

1. Modified KWL chart, created during language invitation
2. Variety of clothing items, such as a bathrobe, a coat, a feather boa, flip-flops, or mud boots
3. Linguistically diverse text (see examples below)

**African American Vernacular English:**

Giovanni, Nikki. 2008. *Hip Hop Speaks to Children: A Celebration of Poetry with a Beat.* Naperville, IL: Sourcebooks.

Greenfield, Eloise. 1974. *She Come Bringin' Me That Little Baby Girl*. New York: HarperCollins.

———. 1978. *Honey, I Love, and Other Poems*. New York: HarperCollins Children's Books.

hooks, bell. 1999. *Happy to Be Nappy*. New York: Jump at the Sun.

McKissack, Patricia. 1986. *Flossie and the Fox*. New York: Dial Books.

Williams, Sherley A. 1997. *Working Cotton*. Orlando: Harcourt Brace.

**Spanish:**

Ada, Alma F. 2004. *I love Saturdays y domingos.* New York: Atheneum Books.

Alarcon, Francisco X. 1997. *Jitomates risuenos: Y otros poemas de primavera/Laughing Tomatoes: And Other Spring Poems.* San Francisco: Children's Book Press.

———. 1998. *Del ombligo de la luna: Y otros poemas de verano/From the Bellybutton of the Moon: And Other Summer Poems.* San Francisco: Children's Book Press.

———. 2001. *Iguanas an la nieve: Y otros poemas de invierno/Iguanas in the Snow: And Other Winter Poems.* San Francisco: Children's Book Press.

———. 2005. *Los angeles andan en bicicleta: Y otros poemas do otoño/Angels Ride Bikes: And Other Fall Poems.* San Francisco: Children's Book Press.

Cisneros, Sandra. 1997. *Hairs/Pelitos: A Story in English and Spanish*. New York: Dragonfly Books.

Garza, Carmen L. 1993. *Cuadros de familia/Family Pictures.* San Francisco: Children's Book Press.

———. 2000. *En mi familia/In My Family.* San Francisco: Children's Book Press.

Medina, Jane 1999. *My Name Is Jorge: On Both Sides of the River*. Honesdale, PA: Boyds Mills.

Perez, Amada I. 2009. *Mi diario de aqui hasta alla/My Diary from Here to There*. San Francisco: Children's Book Press.

*Creating the Chart:*
Blank translation chart

*Closing:*
Translation chart completed earlier in the lesson

# Opportunities for Family–School Partnerships

Language detective notebooks, similar to family dialogue journals (see Chapter 1), are another way to broaden and deepen children's experiences with how language changes based on context, while also inviting families to participate in the conversation. Instead of using this activity to gauge students' understanding of particular standards, have your students use these notebooks to focus on language they hear while they are outside of school. This will remind students that people categorize and change the words they use everywhere, which increases the relevance of grammar study conducted in the classroom; as the children see that people in their homes and communities also code switch, they are more likely to tune in to language study as a tool for effective communication.

Language detective notebooks, a learning tool first documented by Heath ([1983] 1996), are filled with students' independent writing, which makes them a better fit for grade levels in which the children are more independent writers. However, if you wish to use them with younger children, you can enlist the support of family members to help the children write, so they can get their observations of language down on paper. To create a notebook similar to mine for your students, simply copy or handwrite a blank translation chart (with the categories you have already developed with your students) and glue it to the first page of a notebook. Depending on your comfort level and time constraints, you can provide all students with notebooks or just a few students at a time; if you begin with a small group, you can hand the notebooks to a new group after the first group returns them.

You can begin by asking your students what they know about detectives ("They find stuff other people can't!" "Detectives look for clues!"). Next, reveal the blank translation chart that is located within the language detective notebook. Tell your students that with these notebooks, they are going to be language detectives, filling in the chart with words and phrases they hear people say at home or in their community. Talk with the children about what they might listen for and whom they might listen to. You may even want to make lists of these ideas to refer to later if students are having difficulty finding inspiration for the activity. Additionally, discuss with them the intricacies of knowing which column would be the best for recording certain phrases from conversations. For instance, if you are listening to your uncle speak to his employee on the phone, does this count as *family* talk or *other grown-up* talk? Why?

You will want to give your students ample time to be detectives, checking on their progress daily, but not requesting they return the notebooks too soon. Once the children bring them back, gather together to talk about the language students heard in their homes and communities. Even if a small group took home the language detective notebooks, you may wish to include everyone in this conversation, as interesting observations of language could bubble to the surface.

I gave Mack a language detective notebook to try out within our classroom, so he could ask teachers for help in writing down what he heard others say. In the "With Friends" column, Mack wrote, "The book ain't alive—me." Next to this, under "With Other Grown-Ups," he wrote, "The book is not alive—Alex." Mack told his friends and me that this referred to a conversation he'd had with one of our student teachers on the day I gave him the notebook. "Hey! This book ain't alive!" Mack had exclaimed during a lesson on living and nonliving things. Looking at our student teacher, he'd quickly followed his statement with "That's not how you would say it, though." Then, they had written together what Mack thought she would have said in the "With Other Grown-Ups" column. They had decided to write Mack's sentence in the "With Friends" column.

Mack showed his nuanced understanding of how language shifts based on who is speaking and to whom. He showed he was able to use standardized English, although he did not always find it necessary. Our translation charts were proving to be valuable tools that encouraged students to show what they knew without the prescriptive nature of grammar worksheets. It is likely that your own students' responses to a similar activity will reveal equally nuanced results, through the lenses of their unique translation chart categories.

# 3

# LANGUAGE PROBLEM SOLVING |

## Identifying a Problem and Creating a Plan

*Students, as they are increasingly posed with problems relating to themselves in the world and with the world, will feel increasingly challenged and obliged to respond to that challenge.*

Paulo Freire, *Pedagogy of the Oppressed*

Daisy and Lorena were thinking about how they use language while digging through stacks of books. The girls were intrigued by the possibility of coauthoring books in Spanish, English, French, and Korean, and they knew they had connections with people from our extended classroom community who spoke each of these languages.

As we hunted for multilingual texts, Daisy murmured, "It's not fair we only have books in one or two languages. We should have more!" Then she exclaimed, "I have an idea!"

"Daisy, what's your idea?" I asked her.

"That all the Spanish people in the class can write a book," she began. "And then all the English people in the class can write *their* book. And then all the [kids] that wanna do sign language can write the sign language book."

I tried to summarize what Daisy was saying. "So split ourselves up and write different books, instead of all writing the same book in different languages? Interesting!"

Lorena's and Daisy's interest in writing multilingual texts made me wonder: could the co-construction of these books, books that would highlight the linguistic diversity represented within our classroom community, be a project in which we could all engage?

Lorena, Daisy, and I left the library weighed down with books. The girls chattered excitedly about what they wanted to write while I trailed behind them, wondering what a coauthorship book project might look like. Would the other students be interested in something like this? Would families want to be involved? Would colleagues, student teachers, and volunteers be interested in helping us carry out a project of this magnitude?

## Language Problem Solving

Language problem solving is the third building block in language study. The model for language problem solving does not follow traditional teaching methods, where educators present students with information they are expected to learn, and students later demonstrate this learning through a project or test. Instead, language problem solving is more authentically connected to students' interests and existing knowledge, making it a natural partner for language study. Renzulli states, "When content and processes are learned in authentic, contextual situations, they result in more meaningful uses of information and problem-solving strategies than the learning that takes place in overly structured, prescribed classroom situations" (1997, 3). In many ways, language problem solving follows a problem-posing model of education (Freire 1972), where educators and students choose topics of study based on relevance and applicability; this is in contrast to the banking model, where teachers deposit information into the malleable brains of children, without considering the connections between new and existing knowledge. The banking model largely ignores the meaningful expertise children bring to schools and the interest they have in exploring a given topic.

Similar to the Osborn-Parnes model of creative problem solving (Treffinger and Isaksen 2005), language problem solving focuses on using authentic learning experiences to tackle real-life problems. You and your students (1) identify problems and explore the challenge at hand (asking questions and seeking clarifying information when necessary), (2) create a plan for addressing your challenge(s), and (3) work together toward a solution. The main difference is that language problem solving is distinctly language oriented.

## Identifying a Problem

Help children identify a problem that carries weight and relevance. According to Renzulli (1997), a "real-life problem" of this nature must meet the following characteristics:

1. Students must be interested in the problem academically but also *emotionally*—it should be personal to them and to their lives.
2. There should not be an already existing solution to the problem at hand.
3. Students' solution to the problem should involve the dissemination of new information or products that will "change actions, attitudes, or beliefs on the part of the targeted audience" (Renzulli 1997, 2).
4. Students' solution should be directed toward a real audience.

While your class is engaging in a language invitation and creating translation charts, questions or problems will arise. Begin by verbalizing the problem or question students have posed, and ask the whole class if they are interested in helping the initial questioners solve the problem. Then your students can either accept or reject the challenge of finding a solution to this problem. If they accept it, they can begin to brainstorm ways to address it. If they reject it, continue posing problems students identify until the class shows genuine interest in pursuing it.

In my class, our school's enrichment teacher, Katherine Brown, worked with me and my students in each step of the problem-solving process. Is there a teacher, a student's family member, or another classroom volunteer who might partner with you to roll out this project? His or her knowledge and support will be invaluable!

In my first-grade classroom, the question that Daisy and Lorena asked (Why aren't there more multilingual and multidialectal books in our library, and can we do something to change this?) kept coming up. I presented Daisy and Lorena's general problem to the group, adding a few concerns that other students had voiced throughout our language study (see **Figure 3.1**).

FIGURE **3.1**
First-Grade Language Problem Solving Chart

## Our Problem

We discovered a problem with our books!

Most of them are written in English, and lots of us speak Spanish. Not only that, but we know there are lots of different ways to speak English, and books usually show only one way.

We'd also like to see books that are written in languages like French, sign language, and more.

**So what can we do?**

After I read our proposed problem aloud, students shared possible solutions.

"If there's just only English books," Naldo stated, "we can do the same of that with Spanish books." Naldo proposed we could solve this problem by translating English books into Spanish.

Sandra suggested we translate books we already owned into different languages, and Jorge shared that his sister showed him how to use Google Translate to write words in Chinese. "Maybe we can do that?" he asked. The children erupted in excited chatter at this, as they had long been fascinated by Chinese characters.

We were off and running. Children wove familial and communal threads into the discussion. Jorge and Joseph volunteered their siblings to help us with Google Translate, and other students suggested we ask a classroom volunteer to help us write a book in French.

In the end, our class decided to write multilingual and multidialectal books (one in French, one in Spanish, and one in African American Vernacular English) to place in the library.

In Konni Stagliano's third-grade class, the students wondered why multiple languages even *existed* in the world—what were the origins of language, and why don't we all speak the same one? Konni began by revisiting the language invitation chart they had created (see **Figure 3.2**).

FIGURE **3.2**
Third-Grade Language
Invitation Chart

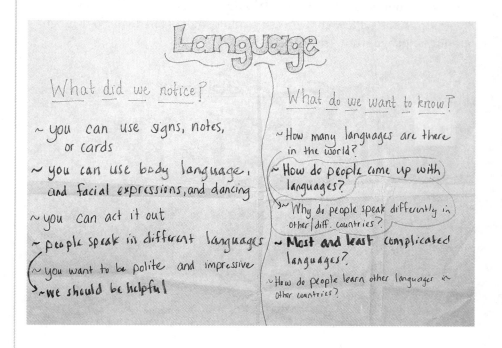

CELEBRATING DIVERSITY THROUGH LANGUAGE STUDY

After reading through the questions students had posed, she pointed out their question about the origins of language. "You all seemed very interested in this," she said. "And it came up when your friends in other classrooms were talking about language, too! This made me wonder: would any of you be interested in researching the origins of language and presenting what you find to the rest of the class?"

A few hands shot into the air, and the class decided this small group would research the origins of language and then present their findings to the class. The students who volunteered were already comfortable with independent research, and Konni knew they would have ample time to complete the project during their centers. In this case, there was less need to create a plan because of the straightforward nature of the project itself.

Did Konni's class' problem meet the four criteria of a real-life problem? Although Konni suggested the product itself (shared research), she did so because the children had already shown significant interest in the topic—and the resource of time was limited.

Take a page from Konni's book—follow your gut as you move forward in a language problem solving project, as you know your students, your available resources and time, and your comfort level regarding the scope of your project. Paying attention to this, and sometimes deviating from the suggested guidelines, will help you ensure the class follows your project through to completion, and that you and your students remain interested and engaged in it throughout!

## Creating a Plan

After you and your students settle on a problem or question about language, it is time to create a plan to address it. Based on the needs and independence levels of your learners, and the time constraints within your classroom, this plan can be as detailed or as general as you would like. The purpose of the plan is to provide you and your students with a functional map for carrying out the goals of your project.

### ◻ Exploring

Start by developing background knowledge. Depending on your students' familiarity with the problem, you may want to provide them with resources to conduct research. Share a variety of options for gathering information (e.g., books, websites, blogs, magazines, encyclopedias, dictionaries). Older children can explore on their own or in groups, while younger children might benefit from a read-aloud or guided exploration of resources. These resources should not spell out your students' actions in a prescriptive way; instead, they should encourage creativity in solving the problem at hand. Give the children time to explore the materials, reminding them that these artifacts might spark ideas for how to move forward. A simple statement like "Let's see if these books/videos/resources can help us think about how we can solve our problem" is a good way to begin this exploratory process.

In my first-grade classroom, we read aloud *The Storyteller's Candle* (González 2008). We learned that the children, their families, and the librarians in the book came together to ensure all community members had access to books. As we read, we discussed the connection between this book and the possible directions for our own project. When Sandra noticed I was reading words in Spanish, I said, "Yeah, they put some Spanish in the English part of the book. Maybe that's something we could do." When Mack observed that the book was "learning everybody Spanish," I responded by saying, "This book *is* teaching everyone Spanish! Yeah, Mack! I wonder if our book can do that, too! Let's see." Throughout the reading, I tried to provide students with the necessary support to co-construct a long-term project while maintaining their interest in the project itself.

## ❑ Brainstorming

Once you feel your students are ready, you can brainstorm solutions (although it is likely the children began to do this while exploring the resources you distributed). It is important that all students are an active part of the brainstorming process and that their voices are heard. You may wish to achieve this through any of the following activities:

- a large-group discussion, where every child has a chance to share
- small-group discussions, where group members report out their ideas
- think–pair–share talks, where partners take turns discussing and sharing their thoughts
- sticky-note writing, where each child records his or her ideas and sticks them to a large chart to share with the group

Be prepared for a variety of responses, as your students will likely be quite creative in identifying solutions. In each case, be sure to record students' ideas for future reference. Consider using a chart to sort these ideas into actions for the beginning, middle, and end of your plan (see **Figure 3.3**).

FIGURE **3.3**
Problem-Solving
Planning Chart

| Solving Our Problem: Making a Plan! | | |
|---|---|---|
| Beginning | Middle | End |
| | | |

After each student received a large sticky note to record possible solutions, my first graders eagerly spread out around the classroom to write.

"Mack, what do you think could solve our problem?" I asked.

Looking up at me, he responded, "I'm gonna draw a library with people in it, and I'm gonna make a sign that some English people can come in with Spanish people."

When I asked Michael what he was drawing, he told me he wanted to solve our problem by telling everyone they were free to go to the library, "because they'd have the same language" as the books within its walls.

"Hmm, OK," I replied. "So what languages could we put in our books?"

"French," he began, naming the home language of a classroom volunteer from Haiti. "And Philadelphia English, and then British," he continued. I was interested that he mentioned different ways to speak English, as I was hopeful we would move toward contextualizing characters' use of words even within the English language. This would allow us to examine registers based on relationships and the formality of characters' situations, which we could then apply to our own linguistic lives (Gee 2011).

When I asked Daisy to explain her sticky note, she offered up a paper divided into four equal sections. She had written her ideas for different books in each one, which she described to me in detail. "All the Spanish people in the class can write a book, and then all the English people in the class can write their book. And then other teachers can write a book in French, and then all the people that want to do sign language can write the sign language book." The words flowed from her, a waterfall of possibilities; she had planned our entire unit, solving our problem by dividing up tasks and having groups write multiple books in familiar languages. "And have teachers that can speak the languages in each group. Mr. Avila can be right here, or the Spanish teachers. And you can be here, and Ms. Candace and Ms. Hanover can write the French book."

Daisy had figured everything out. She had taken her original problem, combined it with what she knew about the children and teachers in our school, and taken notes from the characters' actions in our book. The result was a plan that just might work.

### ◻ Sharing

After brainstorming solutions to your problem, you'll be ready to record these possibilities on a chart like the one in **Figure 3.3** or one of your own design. By sorting students' ideas chronologically, based on when each could be plugged into your emerging project, you and your students will see how they fit together and which suggestions might be clustered into one, making it easier to recognize the connections between ideas.

After my first graders placed their sticky notes on our chart, we shared each one aloud. (See **Figure 3.4** for a representation of the sticky notes my students wrote.)

Most students wanted to create books in multiple languages, but they also shared ideas about including families and teachers as well as having language celebrations where we would invite community members to hear us read our books aloud or perform them as plays. The children had co-constructed their project to organically include three sections: (1) beginning (*planning*), (2) middle (*doing*), and (3) end (*sharing*). The gray highlights in the chart show some of the ideas about which the children were most excited. They wanted to prepare for and *plan* to write books in many languages, including Spanish, by speaking to one another in multiple languages. Then they wished to *write* books in a few of these languages and *share* them within a library setting. Finally, the children wanted to *celebrate* the books by inviting family and community members to see their books before we placed them in the library. This was a big plan, bringing together many of our language study's overarching themes of validating linguistic diversity, sharing our languages with others, and building on our background and experiences to learn new content.

FIGURE **3.4**
Planning–Doing–Sharing Chart

| Solving Our Problem: Making a Plan! | | |
| --- | --- | --- |
| Planning | Doing | Sharing |
| Beginning | Middle | End |
| Speak in lots of languages.<br><br>Chinese<br><br>English<br><br>Spanish<br><br>French<br><br>Sign Language<br><br>We can bring people in our classroom. | We can go to the book store after school to get Spanish books.<br><br>We can make a library with books in other languages.<br><br>We can make a puppet show play that we can turn into a movie.<br><br>We will need to:<br>• check on google translate<br>• work in groups<br>• make resumes | We can put our books in the library.<br><br>We can have a celebration about language.<br><br>Circle with invitations Friday–send home |

Big Idea: Like your skin is a part of your body, your voice (language) is also an important part of you! You should be comfortable with yourself and your language!

No one understood this better than Michael. Thinking back to a previous class conversation about the civil rights movement, Martin Luther King Jr., and Rosa Parks, he said, "I think language is a lot like skin color. When Martin Luther King Jr. was alive, people were treated differently because of their skin color, and people with dark skin weren't allowed to do as much as people with light skin. It wasn't fair."

"That's true, Michael," I responded. "We have talked a lot about that in our class."

Michael continued, "That's just like language. It's not fair that only some people's language is in books. All people should have books that they can read. Language makes you important and special, and that's just like skin color."

I was reminded of Lisa Delpit's powerful words: "Does it not smack of racism or classism to demand that students put aside the language of their homes and communities to adopt a discourse that is not only alien but has often been instrumental in furthering their oppression?" (1994, 297). I sat in front of Michael, a bit awestruck. "Most adults don't recognize this correlation," I wrote later that day in my teaching journal. "And if I'm being honest with myself, I'm not sure I did either, before this moment (at least not so directly)!"

This became our big idea, and we wrote it across the bottom of our organizational chart. The connection Michael made, and the overarching theme he urged us to consider, reminded his classmates and me that our language study validated an important part of our identity. This project became more than trying to identify and discuss differences in language; it was about highlighting and celebrating linguistic diversity.

## How and When: Language Problem Solving Across Grades

In **Figure 3.5**, you'll find additional guidance on language problem solving. Remember that sentences in bold indicate changes I suggest based on age or independence levels. Modify these ideas in any way you see fit.

Giving all students time to ponder these questions individually as they participate in this quick write will ensure that more voices are prepared and ready to respond when you move to small- or whole-group discussion. Additionally, the quality and depth of ideas are likely to increase right away, as the children will have already begun to consider the details of their ideas.

FIGURE **3.5**
Language Problem
Solving Across Grades

| Kindergarten and First Grade |
| --- |

***Structure:***
Language Problem Solving,
Part 1: Identifying a Problem
and Generating a Solution

- Post a language-related problem, identified earlier by a student or group of students, on a large chart.

- As a whole class, engage in a discussion regarding whether this is a problem the children are interested in addressing. Ask questions like these:
  1. Do you agree this is a problem? Why or why not?
  2. Do you think it is possible to do something about it? Why or why not?
  3. Would you like to try? Why or why not?

- As a class, the students will either decide to move forward in pursuing a solution to the problem or decide they are not interested in the given topic.
  *If they remain interested:* Tell them you will begin to formulate a plan to address the problem in an upcoming lesson.
  *If they are not interested:* There are two options. You can encourage students to be on the lookout for a language-related issue they would like to address and come back together to discuss it when this occurs. Or you can ask the children if there are other problems (or versions of this one) they are interested in solving.

***If you identified a problem, move on to*** . . .
Language Problem Solving,
Part 2: Creating a Plan

- Open by reminding your students of the problem they decided to pursue.

- If necessary, present your students with resources to familiarize themselves with the content and/or to help them brainstorm possible solutions. These resources might include websites, books, magazines, encyclopedias, or dictionaries.

- As a whole class, explore these materials. Ask guiding questions, such as
  1. How do you think this book/magazine/ website could help us solve our problem?
  2. It's interesting to think about what this book/magazine/ website is doing with language. I wonder if we could do something like that?

CELEBRATING DIVERSITY THROUGH LANGUAGE STUDY

| Second and Third Grades | Fourth, Fifth, and Sixth Grades |
|---|---|
| • Post a language-related problem, identified earlier by a student or group of students, on a large chart. | • Post a language-related problem, identified earlier by a student or group of students, on a large chart. |
| • As a **whole class or in small groups, each with an identified group leader,** engage in a discussion regarding whether this is a problem the children are interested in addressing. Ask questions like these:<br>1. Do you agree this is a problem? Why or why not?<br>2. Do you think it is possible to do something about it? Why or why not?<br>3. Would you like to try? Why or why not?<br>4. **If so, how will we acquire the resources necessary to do this work?** | • **Ask each student to write down his or her thoughts on the following questions:**<br>1. Do you agree this is a problem?<br>2. Do you think it is possible to do something about it? Why or why not?<br>3. Would you like to try? Why or why not?<br>4. **If so, how will we acquire the resources necessary to do this work?**<br>• **Then, as a whole class or in small groups, each with an identified group leader, engage in discussion around students' written answers to the questions.** |
| • As a class, the students will either decide to move forward in pursuing a solution to the problem or decide they are not interested in the given topic.<br><br>*If they remain interested:* Tell them you will begin to formulate a plan to address the problem in an upcoming lesson.<br><br>*If they are not interested:* There are two options. You can encourage students to be on the lookout for a language-related issue they would like to address and come back together to discuss it when this occurs. Or you can ask the children if there are other problems (or versions of this one) they are interested in solving. | • As a class, the students will either decide to move forward in pursuing a solution to the problem or decide they are not interested in the given topic.<br><br>*If they remain interested:* Tell them you will begin to formulate a plan to address the problem in an upcoming lesson.<br><br>*If they are not interested:* There are two options. You can encourage students to be on the lookout for a language-related issue they would like to address and come back together to discuss it when this occurs. Or you can ask the children if there are other problems (or versions of this one) they are interested in solving. |
| • Open by reminding your students of the problem they decided to pursue. | • Open by reminding your students of the problem they decided to pursue. |
| • If necessary, present your students with resources to familiarize themselves with the content and/or to help them brainstorm possible solutions. These resources might include websites, books, magazines, encyclopedias, or dictionaries. | • If necessary, present your students with resources to familiarize themselves with the content and/or to help them brainstorm possible solutions. These resources might include websites, books, magazines, encyclopedias, or dictionaries. |
| • As a whole class **or in small groups,** explore these materials. **As you circulate,** ask guiding questions, such as<br>1. How do you think this book/magazine/ website could help us solve our problem?<br>2. It's interesting to think about what this book/magazine/ website is doing with language. I wonder if we could do something like that? | • As a whole class **or in small groups,** explore these materials. **As you circulate,** ask guiding questions, such as<br>1. How do you think this book/magazine/website could help us solve our problem?<br>2. It's interesting to think about what this book/magazine/ website is doing with language. I wonder if we could do something like that?<br>3. **How does the work discussed in this book/ magazine/website compare with the work we want to do to solve our problem? What information in this resource is useful for our project and us? What information in this resource is *not* useful for us?** |

*(continues)*

FIGURE **3.5**
Language Problem
Solving Across Grades
(*continued*)

| **Kindergarten and First Grade** |
|---|

Language Problem Solving,
Part 2:  Creating a Plan
(*continued*)

- After exploring the materials, ask the children to record and/or state their solutions to the issue they have identified. They can do this in small groups with a designated leader or individually on large sticky notes. **Emergent writers can use pictures to record their ideas and can dictate the details to be recorded by an adult.**

- Display the planning chart (see Figure 3.3, or create your own), and tell the children you will be using their ideas to plan out their strategy for solving the problem from beginning to end.

- Ask each student to share his or her solution with the class. If students used sticky notes, cluster similar ideas together on your chart. If they are verbally sharing, use the chart to write down a summary of each student's idea. In each case, ask the children in which section you should record the proposed solution.

- As a class, come to consensus regarding the final plan for addressing the problem. Work to include as many of your students' ideas as possible.

- Summarize the students' plan, highlighting the main components. Tell the children they will be carrying out their plan in the coming weeks.

| **Kindergarten Through Sixth Grade** |
|---|

**Time Allotment:** Language Problem Solving, Part 1
Twenty minutes

**Time Allotment:** Language Problem Solving, Part 2
Forty to sixty minutes
- Exploration (optional): twenty minutes
- Brainstorming: twenty-five minutes
- Sharing: fifteen minutes

**Materials:** Problem-Solving Planning Chart (see Figure 3.3)

**Explore:**
1. Supporting resources (optional and varied, depending on student needs and interests)—likely to be some assortment of applicable books, websites, magazines, and encyclopedias

**Brainstorm:**
1. Problem-Solving Planning Chart (see Figure 3.3)
2. Large sticky notes, one for each child (optional)

**Share:**
1. Completed Problem-Solving Planning Chart (for example, see Figure 3.4)

| | |
|---|---|
| • After exploring the materials, ask the children to record and/or state their solutions to the issue they have identified. They can do this in small groups with a designated leader or individually on large sticky notes. **Emergent writers can use pictures to record their ideas and can dictate the details to be recorded by an adult.** | • After exploring the materials, ask the children to record and/or state their solutions to the issue they have identified. They can do this in small groups with a designated leader or individually on large sticky notes. |
| • Display the planning chart (see Figure 3.3, or create your own), and tell the children you will be using their ideas to plan out their strategy for solving the problem from beginning to end. | • Display the planning chart (see Figure 3.3, or create your own), and tell the children you will be using their ideas to plan out their strategy for solving the problem from beginning to end. |
| • Ask each student to share his or her solution with the class. If students used sticky notes, cluster similar ideas together on your chart. If they are verbally sharing, use the chart to write down a summary of each student's idea. In each case, ask the children in which section you should record the proposed solution. | • Ask each student to share his or her solution with the class. If students used sticky notes, cluster similar ideas together on your chart. If they are verbally sharing, use the chart to write down a summary of each student's idea. In each case, ask the children in which section you should record the proposed solution. |
| • As a class, come to consensus regarding the final plan for addressing the problem. Work to include as many of your students' ideas as possible. | • As a class, come to consensus regarding the final plan for addressing the problem. Work to include as many of your students' ideas as possible. |
| • Summarize the students' plan, highlighting the main components. Tell the children they will be carrying out their plan in the coming weeks. | • Summarize the students' plan, highlighting the main components. Tell the children they will be carrying out their plan in the coming weeks. |

# Opportunities for Family–School Partnerships

Home visits. I know this is an overwhelming prospect, but please don't shut the book or skip ahead to a new chapter just yet! As you and your students continue your language study, family perspectives on language will be an invaluable resource. From the opening language invitation until now, your focus has become increasingly unique, representing your students and their linguistic backgrounds while also expanding the ways they use language. As your classroom community works to address a personal linguistic issue, it is all the more important to involve families in your conversations around language and its use in the world. After all, who knows the linguistic struggles, challenges, and successes of your students better than those with whom they have experienced each of these?

Implementing home visits is one way to deepen school–home connections while also increasing the relevance of your problem-solving project. Home visits offer an opportunity for extended conversations around language use. During home visits, teachers and families talk in a comfortable setting, get to know one another, discuss individual children's needs, and share what is going on in the classroom and at home.

This can be an intimidating prospect for both parties involved, as teachers may be uncomfortable in another person's space, and families may feel their child's teacher will judge them, their home, or their way of life. I know both families and teachers who are quite reluctant to share this intensely personal space. Home visits, then, are not for everyone, and they cannot be forced upon families or teachers who would prefer not to engage in this way. However, visiting families in an informal and comfortable setting can be a powerful catalyst for learning about one another, and this richness has the potential to outweigh any initial uneasiness. Not only can you speak more freely while seated on couches and poring over family photos, but home visits also provide the chance for educators to learn about families' funds of knowledge (González, Moll, and Amanti 2005). Funds of knowledge are those areas of expertise held by family members. Maybe you'll learn that a child's uncle is a carpenter and is interested in building a small stage for your readers theatre productions. Or you might find out that one student's mother and father immigrated to the United States from Guatemala, and they are willing to share artifacts during a social studies unit. For the purposes of language study, you might learn that one child's parent is teaching a neighbor how to speak Spanish, in exchange for lessons in English, which is fodder for classroom discussion on the power and relevance of learning to speak multiple languages and dialects. In short, if you are interested in building your language study (or other curriculum) from the perspectives, insights, and background knowledge of your students' families, home visits are a powerful way to bring down the barriers between children's home and school lives.

While connections you make during home visits are often deep and complex, the process of planning and engaging in them is quite simple:

1. Send families a letter to explain what a home visit is. If they are willing to participate, ask them to return a signed form with dates and times they are available to meet (see **Figure 3.6** for a sample letter). You do not need to visit every student's family all at once. Instead, you might focus on a small group of families each weekend, spreading out your visits across a time span that is doable for you. If the process is overwhelming, you'll be less likely to follow it through to completion—and you may miss out on valuable information families are sharing because of sheer exhaustion! So, do what you can to make the experience enjoyable and sustainable.

2. Prepare a few questions, but make every effort not to treat the visit like an interview or information session. The best home visits feel like conversations

FIGURE **3.6**
Sample Home Visit Letter

Dear Families,

Our class is in the midst of a language study, where we think about how we speak in different places and to different people. We have realized we speak differently to our friends than to our teachers, and that the words in books often sound different from the words we use in conversations. This is helping us as readers, writers, and speakers!

Through our discussions, we have learned that our class is very interested in [describe your language problem solving project here]. The children want to know what you know about this topic and about how you use language. Instead of asking you to come to the school, I would love to come visit you at your house, if you are willing. It would give us the chance to talk about our language study and about any questions you might have.

Please fill out and send back the bottom portion of this form to tell me if you are interested in a home visit. Thank you in advance. I hope to hear from you soon!

Sincerely,

_____

- - - - - - - - - - - - - - - - - - - - - - - - - - - - - - - - - - - -

I, _____, am/am not (circle one) interested in a home visit to talk about my child's language study and how I use language.

If you *are* interested, please fill out the following:

Some dates and times I am available are:

and are reciprocal in nature—they should be as beneficial and useful for families as they are for you. If you're making a home visit a part of your language study, you might begin by explaining what language study is and how you'd like children to share their language backgrounds. Be prepared to answer any questions parents might have about this process. You can also ask about a family's language background or about any code-switching experiences they have had. Families might also share what they wish for their children to learn about language. Take notes during these conversations, so you have a record of your discussion; however, try to avoid bringing a laptop or tablet, as it sets up a formal boundary that is contrary to the conversational nature of a home visit.

3. After the visit, reflect on what you learned about the family. What is their language background? What are their hopes for their child, within the context of language study or beyond? What funds of knowledge might they bring to the table? Further, how can you integrate what you learned about the family's background and perspective into your language study? Maybe it's as simple as finding a book written in both English and French to send home with a child whose parents are from Haiti, or making the effort to translate school or classroom notices. Or maybe you connected with a child's mother who is interested in helping you in the classroom. The gap between a child's home and school lives is likely to shrink as you value and respect each person's background in relevant ways.

Often, discussions that occur during home visits will reveal unexpected information, the value of which cannot be overstated. This was certainly the case during a conversation Walter Avila and I once had with two of my students' mothers. The women were concerned their children were not speaking in multiple languages enough in school, because Lorena and Hector sometimes confused the order of words in Spanish sentences. They demonstrated the children's difficulty for us, saying, *"En Español, es familia grande. ¡En Ingles, es grande familia!"* They teased me about my language being backward, saying the English way of ordering our sentences was "wrong" in comparison with their Spanish sentences. Walter laughed as he translated this part, as he had also teased me about my "backward" way of speaking. Each of them knew that, while it was important for their children to learn English in school, it was equally important for them to maintain their ability to speak Spanish.

The women preferred their children speak Spanish *and* English in school, as did other families in our class. This information validated and supported the direction of our problem-solving project. When Lorena and Daisy lamented the fact that there were too many English-only books in the library, and when the children and I put a plan into place to write multilingual and multidialectal books, the voices of these mothers entered into our classroom discussion. The children were interested in capitalizing on the funds of knowledge present in their communities as they worked to make their languages visible within our school space (González, Moll, and Amanti 2005).

# 4

# LANGUAGE PROBLEM SOLVING |

## Taking Action and Reaching Beyond the Classroom Walls

I want to write about how there aren't enough Spanish books in our library," Naldo stated while our class was brainstorming topics for our family dialogue journals one morning (see Chapter 1 for details on how to implement FDJs). Hector and Christopher nodded, showing an interest in this as well. The three boys, all of whom spoke Spanish at home, settled on this as their FDJ focus.

Hector was worried that the "bad man" on the phone would force him and his family to move away because they spoke Spanish (see the Introduction). In that moment, Hector's language was silenced. Since then, Hector had engaged in multiple language study activities: a language invitation, translation charts, and the planning phase of our solution to a language-based problem. Now, it seemed Hector was ready to take back his home language and to consider how his community could engage in Spanish *more* often, instead of less.

The boys walked, with family dialogue journals and pencils clutched in their hands, to claim a table around which they could write. Hector had soon filled up a page with text (see **Figure 4.1**).

What is most striking about Hector's entry is the way he privileged his home language over English. By saying he was learning about *Spanish* books, and that some Spanish books have English and some Spanish books don't have English, he made the primary focus his family's home language. From his vantage point, we should examine texts from the perspective of whether or not the author wrote them in Spanish. As he simply stated, "we want[ed] more Spanish books."

In the midst of studying language through translation charts, and comparing the ways we used words based on context, the children also thought critically about the representation of their own home languages. When they felt underrepresented, Hector and his friends voiced their concerns, making clear their home languages were important to them and *worthy of being connected to school*. The students' wish to include Spanish in more books, and to share these books with others, showed that their interest in studying language, and in pursuing a solution to a communally identified problem, was significant. Language study, then, was the vehicle through which they could study both how to use words in context and how to brainstorm resolutions to relevant issues.

FIGURE **4.1**
Hector's Journal About Language

Dear family,

We are learning about Spanish books. Some Spanish books has English. Some Spanish book don't has English. We want more Spanish books. I can go to different places speak language. How do people speak language?

## Action Plan: Bringing Language Problem Solving to Life

At this point, you and your students have identified a language-related problem and created a loose plan to address this problem. Now you need to put your plan into action! In this chapter, I will discuss how your students' action-oriented plan can sustain interest while also remaining linked to grade-level standards and goals (see the fourth language study building block). Since your classroom's solution will be uniquely your own, use the action plan, guides, and organizers here to help keep track of your progress.

### Planning the Details

A lot can happen in the process of a language study project. Although it may feel daunting at first, keep in mind that the project will include only what you and your students *can* and *wish to* include. While laying out your unique action plan, consider the following:

1. Necessary Steps: Although your students took the lead in identifying a problem and solution, you will need to provide support to help them reach their goal. What are the necessary concrete steps and lessons? If your solution involves writing books or pamphlets, or

creating presentations to share with the community, how will you accomplish this? If your solution focuses on research, how will your students conduct research and share what they find?

2. Standards and Content Alignment: Consider the overarching goal(s) of your project, as well as the detailed steps you have identified. What are the grade-level standards that are already supported by and taught through this project? What grade-level standards *could* be addressed, with a little tweaking of the project? Some of these standards will focus on language, but you might also find that your work will address standards in reading, writing, or other subject areas.

3. Time: How much time do you have to devote to this project? Break it down into small chunks (daily or weekly), and divide lessons based on this commitment, as you feel comfortable.

4. Resources (People): Are there family members, teachers, or other volunteers you would like to partner with as you carry out your plan? Are you thinking creatively about how to include people with a wide array of work and home commitments, designing options for activities they could complete at their own pace and at different times of the day? Carefully considering how best to include multiple stakeholders in the project will help ensure its sustainability.

5. Resources (Materials): What materials do you need to gather before beginning, and where will you get them?

6. Ongoing Language Study Activities: Your problem-solving project will require attention and planning, but you don't have to drop other language study activities during this time. If you are still engaging in translation charts with your students, make a note that you will continue to do so during your project. If you have been following another curriculum for language and grammar study, as part of your school requirements or for personal preference, be sure to set aside time for this as well.

Use the Action Plan Guide (see **Figure 4.2**) to help gather your thoughts. Or, if another organizer or system will work better (sticky notes on the wall, chart paper on the ground, etc.), create your own! The important thing is to make sense of the nuts and bolts of your project.

## ❑ First grade

My students were immediately invested in creating their multilingual books, so we worked to create a plan. First, we voted on the three languages for our books. The children decided to write one book in English (paying particular attention to the register used between characters with different relationships), one in French, and one in Spanish. English and Spanish represented primary home languages. Two of our classroom volunteers spoke and wrote French. Although the children had an interest in Chinese, we quickly realized we did not have the expertise to translate a text from or to this language.

Next, the children picked their groups, writing down their top two language choices on a sheet of paper. The adults also divided into three groups. Our small book groups decided to follow a similar schedule:

- Week 1: Students and teacher(s) brainstormed their book's topic and began to create a graphic organizer showing what would happen at the beginning, middle, and end of their story.
- Week 2: Students and teacher(s) finished creating their graphic organizer.
- Weeks 3–5: Students and teacher(s) collaboratively created the text for their story (in English), with the teacher leader writing the final word choice on a chart for all to see.
- Weeks 6–7: Teacher led students in translating their text. In the Spanish and French groups, students offered the words they knew in each language, while their teacher leader filled in gaps. There was more linguistic expertise in the Spanish group, since many students' home language was Spanish, and because of this we believed they would take more of the lead than those students in the French group. In the English group, translation involved carefully analyzing dialogue between characters and deciding if it needed to be altered based on context (relationship or place).
- Week 8: Students and teacher(s) illustrated the final copy of their text. The medium for these illustrations was up to the students, and could have involved paint, colored pencils, crayons, or cutouts of construction paper.

We all agreed the creation of this text would cover first-grade standards on engaging in collaborative writing, creating a narrative with a clear beginning, middle, and end (weeks 1–5), and using language appropriate for a particular purpose or audience (weeks 6–7).

## ◻ Third grade

Konni Stagliano began her language study late in the year, and by the time her students were ready to create an action plan, there were only a few weeks left before summer vacation. She decided on an informal, small-scale research project because of the time constraints. The small group of interested students completed the project during center time, which gave everyone a finite number of hours in which to work. They agreed together that they would research for approximately one week, and at the conclusion of the week, each team would share its findings with the whole class.

This project covered multiple third-grade standards, and it served as a review of content the class had already covered. Specifically, her students read and gleaned information from a variety of informational sources, recorded relevant information to share, and orally reported what they learned about the origins of language (while also answering questions from peers).

## Carrying Out Your Plan

Once you have a plan, it's time to put it into action. Since you have already done the heavy lifting by considering the nitty-gritty details, this is the fun part! Enact your plan lesson by lesson, and reflect on what your students are saying and doing, how the process is unfolding, and whether you need to modify your approach in any way. Reflect on the process using the Action Plan Reflection Chart (see **Figure 4.3**), which builds on the Action Plan Guide (**Figure 4.2**). Consider students' responses to the process as you move forward, and adjust and modify your plan as necessary.

### ❑ First grade

After our initial planning session, the Spanish, French, and English book groups met once a week for one hour per week. Our guiding question to each group was, "So, what do you want to write about?" The children took this inquiry seriously, coming up with multiple book topics and links to language in multiple contexts.

The French book group chose to write a story about a young girl named Shakira, who was a survivor of the 2010 earthquake in Haiti and who was coming to the United States to begin school. They chose this topic after getting to know a classroom volunteer whose family still lived in Haiti and had also survived the quake. Although the children did not know much French, they learned key words from their group's leader and from letters written by their Haitian pen pals.

The Spanish book group chose to write about some young friends who came upon a magic stone that unfairly helped them to score a goal during a soccer game. Together, the characters decided they should get rid of the magic stone and not count the goal they scored with the magic stone's help. The children in this group were active participants both in composing the initial story and in translating it to Spanish.

The English book group based their book on historical figures the children called "world changers." They wanted to include language spoken in multiple contexts. Although the characters spoke entirely in English, their phrasing and sentence structure would change based on where they were and to whom they were speaking. After some creative brainstorming, the children settled on the idea that these world changers would meet a wizard on a ship who could help them travel through time and meet other world changers.

The children knew that some world changers lived during different time periods. The only exceptions were Rosa Parks and Martin Luther King Jr. They knew these two people were familiar with one another because of their collaboration during the civil rights movement. They decided these characters' conversation would take place at the March on Washington, because both Martin and Rosa were present at the march and interacted at some point. This juxtaposition gave the children the opportunity to play a little bit, to imagine what a conversation between Rosa and Martin might have sounded like.

I learned a great deal about students' ideas regarding language in context while we scripted this brief conversation between Martin and Rosa:

> Martin gives his "I have a dream" speech, and Rosa watches it.

> Rosa traveled to Washington, D.C., to meet Martin Luther King Jr. in 1967. "Where have you been?" said Martin. "I have a speech to give, and I want you there so everything can be right."

After cowriting this, I said to the group, "I think we are ready to think about how we can change how our characters are speaking in our book, since we know more about how they actually talked!"

I highlighted a sentence: "Where have you been?"

"I was thinking," I began. "I bet Martin and Rosa knew each other when Rosa refused to leave her seat on the bus, right?"

The students nodded, agreeing with me.

For historical accuracy, the English book group spent time researching when each world changer lived and used this information to decide how and when characters would meet. Michael insisted we know this, so when the world changers interacted, we could determine which characters lived at the same time. I vividly recall Daisy sitting with a book about Abraham Lincoln in her lap, calling out to Lorena, "He lived from 1809 to 1865!" Lorena nodded seriously, carefully penning "1809–1865" on the story map in her emerging script.

When possible, the children also used videos and audio recordings to listen to their world changers speak, and to discuss the differences in phrasing and formality based on context (Was the world changer in a discussion or giving a speech?) and time period (Did the world changer live one hundred years ago or closer to the current time?).

As you complete your own language problem solving project, consider the research and outside information you and your students will need in order to strengthen the quality of your final product!

"Maybe," I ventured, "we could try to use *friend* talk between them, to make it more like real life? I wonder how Martin might have said this sentence to Rosa if he knew her well?"

A few seconds passed, and then a few more. Silence.

"Hmm . . . how about he says to her, 'Where you been?'?" I made this suggestion as a way to get the conversation started. I knew Martin probably would not have said this to Rosa. I was suggesting a phrase I had heard Mack use with Michael when he had arrived late to school, something I'd heard Daisy shout across the playground to her older sister when she'd noticed her sister had emerged later than her classmates. I thought it might spark other thoughts from the students, that it would help them begin to brainstorm. Instead of hearing more ideas, however, I heard laughter. Contagious, loud, roll-on-the-floor, can't-catch-your-breath laughter bubbled up from their little bodies.

We abandoned this topic for the day. I was a bit flabbergasted by their response. Hadn't they recently accepted Ruby Bridges' *friend* talk into their text, suggesting that Bridges respond, "I don't want no more," when George Washington Carver asked if she wanted more peanut butter? I could not figure out what made this instance so different from that one. I came to realize their reaction was not peculiar at all. First, the suggestion came from their teacher, and they were not used to what they had identified as *friend* talk coming from me. Had a student suggested this sentence, they might have considered it. Furthermore, we had all listened to many speeches given by Martin Luther King Jr., committing to memory certain phrases and plastering them to our classroom wall. When we had listened to King's voice through a computer's speakers a few days earlier, he was giving a speech. The day he interacted with Rosa in our text, he was getting ready to give a speech. Formal speeches were the only context in which they had ever heard Martin Luther King Jr. speak.

From the beginning of our language study, I had emphasized the importance of building our understanding of words in use from personal experiences and from our interconnected encounters with the speech of others (Gutiérrez 2008). The only experiences with Martin Luther King Jr.'s use of words the students could draw from, then, came from his speeches. While I was asking the children to consider how King's relationship with Parks might have influenced his word choice, their experiences likely limited their ability to do so.

We continued to write our book in the weeks to come. These sorts of negotiations continued, as the students thoughtfully considered the words each character would use, incorporating both context and their background knowledge into the discussion. For the most part, our entire English book was written in standardized English, with only Ruby Bridges' speech including snippets of African American Vernacular English (one dialect they had consistently identified as *friend* talk). Although the text was not as multidialectal as I had originally anticipated, the children's process of analysis and justification for how each character spoke sustained itself throughout the text's creation. In the end, this process was instructive, as the children wrestled with words in the context of characters' relationships and the places where they were speaking and according to the students' background knowledge about each.

The Spanish and French book groups continued as well. By the end of week 8, we all finished our text and illustrations. Each book was quite different in topic, size, and media used (see the appendixes for the full text of each). They were united, though, in their commitment to share diverse languages and dialects.

## ◻ Third grade

Konni's group of student researchers spent time daily on classroom computers, using the research skills they acquired throughout the year to search for articles or websites that would help them answer their overarching question: How did different languages originally emerge, and why do people speak differently? When a student found something interesting or relevant to the project, he or she recorded those findings on a sheet of notebook paper, titled "The Beginnings of Language," and shared the findings with the group. Their collective excitement quickly grabbed the attention of the other students, who in turn offered their own research assistance, typing in questions to begin new searches and assisting in reading challenging text.

At the conclusion of their week of research, five volunteers shared their findings with their classmates through a verbal presentation. They discussed their research questions and described the steps they each took to find answers—formatting their questions, using a search engine to locate a large number of results, and then filtering through these results to find the most often mentioned and applicable sources. The group summarized their findings for the rest of the class. Interestingly, some of their research suggested it was "God's doing" that brought about language diversity. They pointed to an Old Testament passage:

> Now the whole earth had one language and the same words. And as they migrated from the east, they came upon a plain in the land of Shinar and settled there. . . . The Lord came down to see the city and the tower, which mortals had built. And the Lord said, "Look, they are one people, and they have all one language; and this is only the beginning of what they will do; nothing that they propose to do will now be impossible for them. Come, let us go down, and confuse their language there, so that they will not understand one another's speech." So the Lord scattered them abroad from there over the face of all the earth, and they left off building the city. (Gen. 11:1–2, 5–8, New Revised Standard Version)

This passage showed up in multiple Internet sources, according to the student researchers, and they came to the conclusion that it was one explanation for the diversity in language that now exists. Some of their classmates accepted this, while others were not satisfied with this explanation. Although the conversation was brief, and no particular belief system was prized over another, the research process (which has its own value) opened up opportunities for critical thinking, public speaking and questioning, and the possibility that students would continue their research.

Although Konni was encouraged by both her students' sustained interest in this project and what they learned from it, the class still had lingering questions about why people speak differently. If there had been more time remaining in the year, she decided, she would have extended this research and given the students time to discover more about the differentiation of language and its many uses in a variety of contexts. She envisioned extensions. She could incorporate these findings into reading comprehension activities, discussing with her students why author(s) choose particular words or phrases when creating texts. Her class could analyze whether a shift in word choice would change the message or feel of a text, placing phrases from books into different codes (*family*, *friend*, or *other adult*) and discussing what happens when meaning remains the same but the words are different. Then she could ask students these questions as they engaged in their own writing. Konni also envisioned writing conferences where she would probe individuals to think about the intended audience for their writing or about their use of written dialogue between characters with particular relationships. For example, she might ask, "Would these characters use *friend*, *family*, or *other adult* talk with each other? Are there other phrases you could use to convey this relationship more convincingly?" Or she might say, "You are writing a persuasive letter to your principal. Do your sentences sound like *other adult* talk? If not, what changes could you make in the words you are using?"

As Konni finished this work with her students, she reflected on the spiraling and interconnected nature of language study activities. They moved from an open-ended exploration (language invitation) to focused inquiry within a particular area of interest (language problem solving). Questions from earlier activities led her students to research the origins of language, and these results made her consider how she could use students' continued interest and newfound knowledge to expose them to even more intricacies of language in use. "Discovery of language and its many uses is a continuous learning adventure for us all," she said, "but especially for students just learning how to express themselves orally and within the context of writing." The project opened up a multitude of relevant opportunities for discovery and adventure.

## How and When: Action Plans Across Grades

Since each action plan is different, use the following two organizers to help you think through the details of your plan and its execution. Share, reorganize, slightly alter, or completely restructure these sheets to make them relevant to your students, their families, the teachers in your community, and you.

The Action Plan Guide (see **Figure 4.2**) is designed to provide a framework for the details of your action plan. The Action Plan Reflection Chart (see **Figure 4.3**) is designed to help you reflect as you carry out your action plan.

FIGURE **4.2**
Action Plan Guide

| Project Title: | | |
|---|---|---|
| **Goal or Focus of Project:** | | |
| **Timeline (hours/week):** | | |
| **Steps:** | **Standards Addressed:** | **Resources Necessary (People, Materials):** |
| **1.** | | |
| **2.** | | |
| **3.** | | |
| **4.** | | |
| **Ongoing Language Study Activities:** | | |

FIGURE **4.3**
Action Plan Reflection
Chart

| Steps<br>(These should be the steps from the Action Plan Guide.) | What *successes* have you and your students experienced?<br>(These may be linked to grade-level standards.) | What *challenges* have you and your students faced?<br>(These may be linked to grade-level standards.) | What adjustments or modifications might be needed?<br>(These should be based on your successes and challenges.) |
|---|---|---|---|
| **1.** | | | |
| **2.** | | | |
| **3.** | | | |
| **4.** | | | |

# Opportunities for Family–School Partnerships

Engage families in surveys, in questionnaires, or as editors of your project. Just as you and your students will reflect on your action plan as it unfolds, the children's families can offer valuable insights and reflections on what you are doing and producing.

The most effective modes of family support will vary depending on your project and the goals of your action plan. In my first-grade classroom, families served as editors for our multilingual and multidialectal texts. After we finished drafts of our completed texts in Spanish, French, and English, we sent home paper copies, complete with highlighters and markers for editing ease. Children and families discussed changes they should make. Families who primarily spoke Spanish received copies of our Spanish group's book, families who primarily spoke English received our English group's book, and two French-speaking teachers in our building received our French group's book.

Almost all families responded in some way, and a few families provided very detailed feedback. One English-speaking family told our book group to watch verb tenses and check certain sentence construction. This led to the children's decision to take Ruby's *friend talk* out of the English text, leaving the entire book written in standardized English. Though I was originally disappointed, as the language diversity disappeared with this change, I honored the students' decision. After all, they had engaged in the process of examining, questioning, and celebrating multiple languages and dialects, and I believed this process was the most valuable aspect of our work.

The children were also very invested in the editing process. Hector and Christopher, for instance, continued to edit the Spanish text even after they turned in the assignment. They knelt on the floor, highlighters in hand, to check on one sentence Hector said "sounded funny." I read it aloud to him, and after hearing the sentence in its entirety, he shook his head left to right, saying, "Oh, yeah! That sounds right!" He then wrote "makes sense" underneath his newly highlighted Spanish words, before turning to hand his packet to me.

In the end, each book group had a conversation about families' suggested changes; the students accepted some edits and ignored others. This process brought us one step closer to the completion of each text, and the books were strengthened because our families served as coauthors and editors.

Identify a way for your students' families to contribute meaningfully to your action plan. Whether it's through surveys, questionnaires, text edits, or something else entirely, family members' perspectives can add depth and relevance to an already personal project.

# 5

# CELEBRATING LANGUAGE |

## Sharing with Your Community

"Excuse me, Ms. McCreight?" Michael politely inquired one afternoon, as we all sat working on the illustrations for our multilingual books.

"Yes, Michael?" I asked, looking up from a picture of a time-traveling wizard that Daisy was coloring.

"I know why we're doing this," he said confidently.

"Why we're drawing these pictures?" I probed.

"No, why we are doing *this*," he explained again, now pointing at the books around him. "Why we're making these *books*."

"Why, Michael?" I asked.

"It's for community," he began, "to build a community, and do something to help the community."

"What are we doing for the community here, Michael?" I probed further.

"When people read our books," he went on, "they can see that language can be different, and we can still like people who speak different."

In this short exchange, Michael hit on the very valuable point that different languages are valid and important. It was something we had discussed throughout our language study, as we had translated phrases from *family* to *other grown-up* talk, when we had carefully considered the words we would write in books based on context, and so on.

He also brought up a point shared by other students: people should be reading our books, because our larger community needed to experience multiple dialects and languages in the pages of children's literature.

We were ready, I thought, for a language celebration.

# Language Celebrations: Sharing Your Learning

Language celebrations are a way for you and your students to share what you have learned about language throughout the school year (see the fifth language building block). These celebrations will feel like equal parts *party* and *social action event*. Remember, part of Renzulli's (1997) definition of a real-life problem is that your solution is directed toward an authentic audience. You and your students have designed your problem-solving project with a particular audience in mind, picturing families, teachers and administrators, other children (younger, older, or grade-level peers), or community members as the recipients of your message. Now you will need to think about how you will share this work with your intended audience.

## Planning a Language Celebration

A language celebration can take place in a variety of venues and in a variety of formats. It may be intimate or grand, formal or cozy. You will want to engage your students in the planning process, while keeping in mind realistic parameters. Begin by asking the following questions and see where they lead you:

1. *What do you want to share?*
   This is the most critical consideration, and your responses to all other questions hinge on it. Refer back to the goals of your language-based project. What did you learn or create that you now want to share? The answer will vary based on your project.

2. *How will you share it?*
   You and your students will have to determine the setup and format of the celebration as well as the displays you will use to disseminate the information.

   The presentation format could be any one of the following:

   - Lecture: Audience listens to a presentation together, focused on project artifacts when applicable. Anywhere from a few to all students can actively participate.
   - Small-Group Presentations: Audience rotates in a set amount of time to hear each group share project artifacts and what the students learned.
   - Poster Presentations: Much like poster presentations at academic conferences, small groups, partners, or individual children

display the project's artifacts, and audience members stop in to ask the students questions and to see the project itself.

Next, think about the best way to showcase your project. The language celebration may not be the final home for your project (consider my students' multilingual and multidialectal books, which would eventually live in a local library to be read and shared), but it is one venue through which you can begin sharing your message with the broader community. Your particular project may speak for itself, with audience members engaging with your students and the materials they created to find out more about the topic at hand. Or, if your final project is more abstract, you may need to create a formal presentation to describe your process and conclusions. You could make a presentation with PowerPoint or Prezi and display it on a projector or large poster board (whole group) or on tablets or smaller poster boards (small groups) and have the students explain it to their audience.

3. *Whom will you invite?*

   Consider the target audience for your project, as well as key community (school and home) members who have a stake in the success of the project. Don't forget to invite students' families, as their contribution to students' language use makes them VIPs on this list of stakeholders! Also take into account the space you have for the celebration itself and the logistics of rotations (Is there enough space to move from one small group to another?) and seating (Will audience members and students be able to sit comfortably?).

4. *Where will the celebration take place?*

   Remember to consider audience access. Will the people you invite be able to get there? Depending on your school's neighborhood, consider bus schedules and carpooling arrangements. Some potential locations are your classroom; the school gymnasium; and a community center or park that is central to many families' homes.

5. *When will the celebration take place?*

   Again, consider audience access. When will the people you invite be available (e.g., off work)? This will determine whether the celebration should take place during or after school hours, or if you want to offer multiple "showings" of your celebration.

6. *What other details do you need to consider?*

   ■ Will your intended audience need access to childcare? If so, will you have an area set up for young children to play in?

Or will the entire celebration be appropriate for families with young children to engage in?

- Will you provide refreshments? Snacks are always appreciated and can create a conversational atmosphere. If your celebration takes place over the lunch or dinner hour, consider offering a more substantial spread or suggesting a potluck.

To keep all of this information organized, use the Language Celebration Planning Guide (see **Figure 5.1**).

## Celebrating in First Grade

My first graders and I spent a considerable amount of time planning and prepping our celebration. We invited our families, another first-grade class, and various teachers and community members who had been part of our language study. We settled on a daytime event, held on both Thursday and Friday at different times, in order to accommodate as many audience members as possible. We wrote and sent out invitations, in Spanish and English.

At our celebration, we planned to read our multilingual books as the authors themselves stood nearby to explain the text and how they had come to write it. We wanted to make the room as inviting as possible, so we displayed other examples of children's literature written in French, Spanish, and English. I wrote "Bienvenidos! Bienvenue! Welcome!" on a whiteboard set up on a table by the door and set out prompting sheets, full of questions visitors might ask the students (e.g., Tell me about your book. What did you learn about language when you wrote it? What was your favorite part about creating the book? Why do you think it's important to share these texts with others?). The children and I practiced answering these questions in groups before each day's celebration.

On the morning of the celebration, a palpable buzz hummed throughout the room as soon as the children walked in the door. "My mama is coming!" Mack informed me the second his feet hit the doorway. "She's coming after work! So's my sister!" He was beaming, bouncing up and down on the balls of his feet as he spoke. He tried to hang his backpack on a hook, and in his excitement he completely missed, his bag hitting the floor with a thud. Mack's classmates equaled his energy level, and each time someone mentioned our language celebration, an eruption of voices broke the otherwise quiet of the room.

Finally, it was time. We fanned out, standing in front of freshly laminated books written in English, French, and Spanish, ready to receive our families and friends. The students stood tall and proud, nearly tripping over one another to answer guests' questions. They discussed details about how they constructed each book and the reasons we had created the texts. As each person arrived, voices swelled in the already boisterous space, announcing with excitement another anticipated guest. Children ran to greet family members, pulling them by the hand to their book's table. Other guests received more widespread star treatment, as multiple children, vying for the attention of a beloved classroom community member, rushed forward to lead them to their group's project.

There was Naldo's mother, who read the entire Spanish text to an audience of both English- and Spanish-speaking students. This group of seven children fanned around her, with Naldo in his mother's lap and the rest of the students touching some part of her arm, shoulder, or hand, as she quietly breathed life into the words on every page of their text.

Michael, Mack, Lorena, and Hector told guests, each at separate times, that they were going to take all their books to the library to put a barcode on them so others could check them out. Each child communicated that it was important for us to create these books because we noticed that some libraries do not have many books in languages other than English.

Soon after, I observed Michael shyly smiling up at his mom as she said, "Michael, you realized that the way people are treated badly because they don't speak English is like how African Americans were treated badly because of skin color? You need to tell everyone about that!" Michael stood in the glow of his mother's praise. She realized he inspired our class to work for change, learning from events in history to do so.

In each of these moments, something special happened. Through the sharing of our multilingual books, students and families learned more about one another. The children moved from discussing the beauty of the Spanish language to hearing it spoken aloud by Naldo's mother. They shifted from affecting change primarily in their classroom to spreading news of the beauty of multiple languages to other adults they knew. We entered into a Third Space of learning, which

> has always been more than a celebration of the local literacies of students from nondominant groups; and certainly more than what students can do with assistance or scaffolding. . . . Instead, it is a transformative space where the potential for an expanded form of learning and the development of new knowledge are heightened. (Gutiérrez 2008, 152)

In these moments, students, families, and friends were celebrating local literacies and sharing writing they had accomplished together, but our celebration was more than that. As Gutiérrez describes, it was a space within which students taught their families, where parents ignited renewed interest in words the children had begun to take for granted. We opened ourselves up to an "expanded form of learning" and to "the development of new knowledge." In this space, we found we had transformed into learners with expanded perspectives and experiences.

In all, we welcomed forty-six members of our extended classroom community, all to experience our solution to a linguistic problem we had identified in the world. This translated to forty-six pairs of eyes and ears learning about the reason behind our books, forty-six hearts and minds moved by the work of these children, and forty-six opportunities for our message about the beauty in language diversity to spread to our larger community. We hoped we would "get people doing things," to borrow Michael's words, and the effort made by so many family members and friends to learn about our books gave us hope. Further, the concreteness of our three texts provided staying power for our words, and I was confident in the students' ability to verbalize their conviction about respect for multiple languages and dialects.

## How and When: Celebrations Across Grades

Since language celebrations will vary, it is difficult to provide you with a set list of procedures, materials, necessary people, and time allotments. In **Figure 5.1** you'll find an organizer designed to help you think through the details of your language celebration. Any grade level can use this document. Share, reorganize, slightly alter, or completely restructure this sheet—make it relevant to your students, their families, the teachers in your community, and you.

FIGURE **5.1**
Language Celebration
Planning Guide

| Overarching Goal(s):<br>What do you want to share? | |
|---|---|
| How will you share it? | *Lecture:* |
| | *Small Groups:* |
| | *Poster Presentations:* |
| Whom will you invite? | |
| Where will you celebrate? | |
| When will you celebrate<br>(date and time)? | |
| What other details<br>should you consider? | *Childcare:* |
| | *Refreshments:* |
| | *Other:* |

# Opportunities for Family–School Partnerships

The language celebration is an opportunity to share your students' work with their families and friends. It is also a natural time to think about the successes and challenges of language study. In Chapter 6, I will discuss some concrete ways for you and your students to measure growth and to reflect on the impact of this work; however, as I have noted throughout this text, families will be able to share a unique perspective on the impression of language study. Engage families in feedback around your approach to language study. In doing so, you will gain critical insights as to what worked, what didn't, and what you can do differently in the coming years.

Family members have been speaking to you throughout your language study (in informal conversations, family–teacher conferences, home visits, family dialogue journals, and more). For more targeted feedback, use a reflection questionnaire (see **Figure 5.2** for a sample). You can ask these questions in person or send home written questionnaires. For an in-person conversation, the questions may give you a starting point. As always, though, please reformat or alter these words to fit your needs.

FIGURE **5.2**
Sample Language Study
Questionnaire

Dear Family,

As you know, your child has been engaging in a language study this year. Instead of only studying the rules of grammar and insisting on standardized English all the time, we have been thinking about how we speak and write based on context (*whom* we are speaking to and *where* we are). We have also learned about different ways of speaking and writing by building on the words and phrases we already use to communicate with family, friends, and other grown-ups.

Now, we would like to know what you think about our language study! Thank you in advance for the time you take to fill out this questionnaire!

Sincerely,

_____

1. Has your child talked to you about the language or grammar he/she uses in different places and with different people? If so, what has he/she said?

_____

2. I would love to know what you think of our [fill in with the focus of your action project here] project.

_____

3. What do you think your child learned while participating in this project?

_____

4. Did you learn something about language when you heard about the project or attended our celebration? In other words, did your child's work cause you to think differently about language and how you use it? Or about how you judge others (either positively or negatively) because of the words they use?

_____

5. Do you think that learning how language works in context (e.g., you might speak differently to your friends than to your principal, or you might speak differently while giving a speech than at the dinner table) will benefit your child in the future? Why or why not?

_____

# 6

# REFLECTING | Looking Back to Move Forward

A classroom language study is unique in its very design, an exploration of language based on the context in which a particular teacher and group of students live and learn, buoyed by links to students' experiences and backgrounds. However, there are overarching aspects of language study that, no matter how a particular study unfolds, are critical to ensuring successful interactions and to validating students' home lives and background knowledge. Beyond specific activities, a certain mind-set is necessary to contextualize an oft-*de*contextualized subject matter.

In short, there are big ideas, guideposts past which language study moves forward. Each of these overarching tenets of language study affects academic performance, student and family engagement, and educators' outlook and approach to teaching grammar and language. Where teachers and students feel successful, these central tenets are prominent. Where students and teachers struggle, they may be shaky or underdeveloped. There are fundamental components to a successful language study (see language building block 6):

- conducting formative assessment
- studying context
- seeking progression from concrete to abstract
- making sure power is shared

## Conducting Formative Assessment

Throughout language study, it is critical to consistently reflect on lessons, activities, and projects. Teachers can do so by collecting notes and student work samples and recording information they have gleaned in organizers, evaluating what went well and what they might have done differently. This reflection allows educators to constantly engage with data, to best incorporate the intricacies of their classroom's culture into language study.

These reflections have a direct and immediate impact on classroom practice. While reflecting, teachers determine future activities and next steps. Examining their practice also helps them to compare students' perspectives with their own, as they consider whether students' voices were being heard or whether they were pushing their own agenda or ideology. Through this reflection, educators are better attuned to the needs and interests of their students.

Formative assessment, then, is a critical component to language study. As defined by Black and William, formative assessment refers to "all those activities undertaken by teachers, and/or by students, which provide information to be used as feedback to modify the teaching and learning activities in which they are engaged" (1998, 7). In short, we monitor student progress along the way and respond to it, rather than give end-of-unit tests, assign grades, and move on to new content regardless of students' demonstration of knowledge. In today's standards-based education culture, where students focus on mastery of content across semesters or even an academic year, formative assessment has become a cornerstone of effective instruction.

And it is just good teaching! We should respond to each student where he or she is and based on what that student already knows, in order to decide how and what we expose him or her to next. This is why formative assessment, through continued data collection and reflection on such data, is critical to language study. There are three assessment tools for data collection and reflection you might use during your language study (see **Figures 6.1**, **6.2**, and **6.3**).

## Studying Context

Within language study, studying context and its impact on language choice is crucial. As Andrews stated, "language choices . . . reflect . . . social and professional, formal and informal settings" (2001, 112), and because language study shares this outlook, students and teachers construct categories of language around vast and varied relationships. By using language categories based on the people with whom our students speak, we open up possibilities for categorization that are not as clear when considering only home and school language. When we start by categorizing words based on place, it helps students to see the diverse linguistic demands of specific spaces, but these categories do not always hold up in their actual conversations. For instance, students speak differently on the playground or cafeteria than in more formal classroom discussions, which makes it confusing to explain school language and home language as fixed ways of speaking. By

FIGURE **6.1**
Data Collection Tool for
Translation Charts

| Questions | Translation Chart (Based on previously used children's literature) | Translation Chart (Based on student-created categories) |
|---|---|---|
| 1. Were most or all students able to translate one way of speaking to another, using a consistent dialect or language to represent each category? | | |
| a. *If so*, what contributed to this success (either during this activity or in previous lessons)? | | |
| b. *If not*, what prevented them from being successful (either during this activity or in previous lessons)? | | |
| 2. Did any students say anything that surprised you (either positively or negatively)? | | |
| a. What did they say, and why did this come as a surprise? | | |
| b. How can you structure next year's study to either increase similar responses (if positive) or explore reasons for this response (if negative)? | | |

FIGURE **6.2**
Data Collection Tool
for Language Problem
Solving

1. Were there steps in your project that were *too* planned out? In other words, did you try to control too much?

_____

_____

2. What can you do next year to give up some of this control and allow the process to unfold more naturally?

_____

_____

3. Were there steps in your project that were left up to chance?

_____

_____

4. What can you do next year to ensure a more organized project, while still allowing the process to reflect the backgrounds and interests of your students?

_____

_____

5. Did you address any standards in depth through your project? How did you manage to authentically incorporate standards into a largely student-driven project?

_____

_____

6. Are there standards you could have addressed more fully through your project but didn't? How could you have incorporated these standards into your students' work?

_____

_____

7. Next year, you will have new students with different backgrounds and interests, so your project will be different. What are some general lessons you have learned? How will you approach language study differently next year?

_____

_____

FIGURE **6.3**
Data Collection Tool
for Language Study

1. Across time, what language-based skills or standards did language study help students master most consistently? (Refer to Appendix D.)

   _____

   Why do you think this was the case?

   _____

   Based on your assessment, what language study activities will you continue next year?

   _____

2. Across time, what language-based skills or standards did language study *not* help students master?

   _____

   Why do you think this was the case?

   _____

   Based on your assessment, what changes will you make to language study activities next year?

   _____

3. What were your primary methods of assessment (e.g., writing samples, worksheets, observational notes, audio recordings)?

   _____

   What gave you the *most* information about your students' language learning?

   _____

   What gave you the *least* information about your students' language learning?

   _____

   How can you *increase* the use of the most effective methods of assessment next year?

   _____

4. What information do you wish you had gathered on the Language Study Formative Assessment Guide (Figure 1.5)?

   _____

   How will you include this information next year?

   _____

considering person-based categories, grounded in relationships, in addition to setting, you can create a more nuanced system. Dyson and Smitherman found "there is evidence that children who speak nondominant vernaculars . . . become bidialectal (or bilingual) through interacting in diverse social situations with others who control varied ways with words, and through opportunities to exercise agency over language choices" (2009, 979). By examining language based on relationships, teachers and students engage in these types of linguistic opportunities.

Further, by studying language that is familiar to students, teachers can tap into their prior knowledge much more effectively, significantly increasing the likelihood that the children will retain what they are learning about the intricacies of words in the world. As Campbell and Campbell said, "students . . . bring beliefs and life and academic experiences to the classroom that influence what and how they learn. At times, such prior knowledge facilitates learning by creating mental hooks that serve to anchor instructional concepts" (2008, 7). Language study invites and encourages such anchors, as it asks students to make connections between phrasing and sentence structure that are familiar to them and the use of words in a variety of new or less familiar contexts.

In addition, because the study of language makes relationships a key component of classroom communities through a variety of activities (family dialogue journals, home visits, and classroom visits by families, teachers, and volunteers), space is opened up for students to identify a linguistic issue affecting their extended community. This leads to the possibility of engaging in a unique and highly personal problem-solving project. Because relationships are crucial to the functioning of a classroom community, they are also crucial to identification of a problem worth addressing (Freire 1972). Previous studies on the academic achievement of students engaging in a version of the creative problem-solving process, the model on which language problem solving is based, have found that students increase their ability to think divergently and come up with multiple solutions to problems (Fasko 2000). Researchers like Woolfolk (1998) have found that these results are strengthened when students solve problems that are highly relevant to them. In an educational and professional climate increasingly focused on twenty-first-century skills, it stands to reason that children who have experience with critical thinking and problem solving will be better prepared for both school and work experiences that require them to identify and plan solutions to real-world problems.

# Seeking Progression from Concrete to Abstract

As students and teachers progress through language study, they do not begin with the abstract diagramming of sentences. Instead, they discuss and categorize sentences they have already spoken or heard with their friends, families, and others, adding relevance and familiarity to this process. Then they move on to translate sentences from a familiar book. Only then do teachers ask students to categorize and code switch less familiar sentences from one student-created category to another. James Gee similarly supported language instruction focused on students' prior knowledge, saying,

> There is evidence that focusing learners on the right input at the right time, namely, when they are ready for it and they have practiced in natural settings, is a form of [linguistic] teaching that can succeed. It may be the only kind of overt teaching that can. (1989, 139)

In other words, when studying grammar and language, it is critical for students to experience practice time and for teachers to expose their students to new intricacies in language codes only when they are ready. This process of scaffolding students' learning from their background and experiences is a time-honored and time-tested practice in most subject areas, but one less explored in the teaching of grammar. Language study focuses on "high-connection" lessons that build upon the idea that students' "background knowledge and world view may be derived from personal experience of their community and local area, from their linguistic and cultural heritage, and/or from the media and popular culture" (Curriculum Implementation Unit 2002, 22). As such, children not only feel supported but are also better able to connect new information to existing knowledge, therefore committing it to their long-term memories.

# Making Sure Power Is Shared

A critical component of language study is to share power with students and families. Carrie Secret said, "I am there because an adult has to be with the children, but I try not to have a hierarchy. There needs to be a mutual respect between the teacher and students" (1998, 86). While teachers typically hold the most power in classrooms, and while their expertise is essential to moving classroom learning forward, language study is a platform for instruction that encourages you, your students, and their families to share this power, and for all to become more active participants in the classroom.

Students and teachers share power each time they engage in discussion around questions to which there are no predictable answers. They also share power when they discuss the trajectory of activities and projects, coming together to create artifacts and plan celebrations. This sharing of power leads to a classroom community that is connected and supportive, therefore increasing the likelihood students will feel valued and cared for. According to Maslow's hierarchy of needs (1943), these feelings of love and belonging are not only essential in their own right but also precursors for children's ability to engage in problem-solving activities or to learn new information in school. If children feel their teachers and peers value their ideas, consider their perspectives, and share academic and social power with them, they are more likely to focus on and learn the information at hand.

Teachers and students' families also share power. They do so when families' schedules inform the times and dates of language activities and celebrations. They work together to incorporate and celebrate home languages in curriculum, communicating in families' most comfortable language as often as possible. Families may participate in the language problem solving project as well. As Henderson et al. (2007) have noted, students' academic achievement is positively affected when children and families engage in school- and standards-based projects and inquiries together. Language study's focus on family–school partnerships sets up an environment in which students find an increased connection between school and home, and that is conducive to increased retention of information.

In these ways and more, teachers, students, and families share power. They acknowledge the beauty in one another's backgrounds and knowledge bases, committing to learn *from* and *with* one another (Freire 1972). Through language study, they work together in ways that are not typically part of language and grammar instruction. And in doing so, they increase the likelihood that students will not only recall and remember what they learned about words in their world, but also that they will care about the underlying reasons for such categorization, as they learn the intricacies of negotiating linguistic codes in a variety of places and with a variety of people.

## Final Thoughts and Recommendations

While it is exciting to think about how you and other teachers might incorporate language study into classrooms, individual teachers working for change in grammar instruction will likely face resistance in the form of district- or state-adopted policies and programs. While individual educators, grade levels, or even schools might choose to adopt an open-ended form of grammar instruction, building from students' home languages and prior experiences, children will surely come across teachers, buildings, or tests that do not take into account their understanding of contextualized language, seeing only standardized English as acceptable or appropriate.

While language diversity may lead students to question educational formats that call for a one-size-fits-all mentality, how long can this type of study last without school support? How long, for example, can I expect Michael to share his beliefs about language discrimination if our curriculum does not support these beliefs? How can I expect any of these children to continually link *family*, *friend*, and *other grown-up* talk to their writing and speaking if a classroom conducts only workbook-style grammar study?

Policy change is necessary, toward a reconstruction of grammar study at the district, state, and national levels, if students are to develop a nuanced, long-term ability to navigate effectively between the multiple codes that are part of their daily lives. As Freire said, "many political and educational plans have failed because their authors designed them according to their own personal views of reality, never once taking into account . . . the men-in-a-situation to whom their program was ostensibly directed" (1972, 83). This is often the case with language study, as those creating workbooks and test questions represent the voices of those already in powerful positions, unaware of the implications inherent in underrepresenting the multiple codes children employ every day in speaking to others. Regardless of policy makers' and curriculum and test creators' intentions, we must "think deeply and thoughtfully about the ways in which our use of theory will affect real students in real classrooms . . . , [or] we are neglecting our ultimate responsibility" (González, Moll, and Amanti 2005, 39–40). With this in mind, here are suggestions for grammar instruction that allow for multiple voices and perspectives:

- *Offer consistent, long-term language study.*
  Districts could save considerable amounts of money by choosing to build a grammar curriculum on students' and families' experiences rather than buying into prescriptive grammar studies. And as my student interviews showed, students would still be able to differentiate between more and less formal language, based on context and speakers' relationships. While feeder schools, districts, or even states

would have to consider identifying consistent categories for students to work within across grade levels (e.g., a block of schools would develop their language studies based on the same registers), each could be conceived based on feedback from students, families, and teachers. This would make the categorization of language more applicable to children's everyday lives than disconnected standardized English worksheets.

- *Extend invitations to families.*
  Those of us from SE-speaking backgrounds cannot purport to understand the perspectives and academic hopes of families whose language background is in another language or dialect. If we are to create space in which all students can learn and thrive, we need to blend the expectations of families with those currently upheld in schools and the larger society. If families like Hector's and Christopher's want their children to learn both English and Spanish in school, why might this be so? Reach out to them and ask. If parents like Natalie's want their children to learn SE over AAVE, why is this so? Reach out and ask. What can we learn from one another, if we truly enter into dialogue, and how much better off will the children in our care be for it? Start meaningful dialogue with families around these inquiries, and all involved will more actively participate in the construction of your grammar curriculum.

So, where will you go from here? How might language study inform and influence the way you teach language and grammar in your classroom? What aspects of this approach did you not attempt this time around that you might try in future years? Will you increase your implementation of these or other language activities next year? How will your approach stay the same? How will it change? What concepts within your grade-level standards can be taught through language study, and how can you accomplish this? How can you more effectively bring your students' families into discussions and activities around words in their world?

The answers to these questions are uniquely yours. Try bits and pieces of language study, or embrace it fully, tweaking it to fit your needs along the way. But whatever you do, remember: it is critical that we build upon and learn from our students' out-of-school lives.

These words are familiar.

These words are theirs.

And just as we do in all other subject areas, it is our job to honor their backgrounds while adding tools to their "linguistic toolbox" (Wheeler and Swords 2004, 473). An approach to grammar study that involves discussion, exploration, and social action projects centered on students' lives will inspire interest, purpose, and relevance.

When was the last time you achieved *that* while diagramming sentences?

# APPENDIX A

## First-Grade English-Based Language Problem Solving Group

### World Changers Go Time-Traveling

**Characters:** Rosa Parks, George Washington Carver, Abraham Lincoln, Abraham Lincoln's Friend, Ruby Bridges, Martin Luther King Jr., and the Wizard

Once upon a time, Rosa Parks met a time-traveling wizard on a ship. She told him how she changed the world. Rosa said, "People were separating us on the bus. I had to stop this, so black and white people could sit together. Lots of people boycotted the buses with me."

The wizard said, "What is your wish?"

"Will you build a time machine so I can meet other world changers? I don't know about all world changers. I only know about some of them," said Rosa.

The wizard said, "Yes. I am a wizard for world changers. All you have to do is spin my magic globe and make your wish!"

Rosa spun a magic globe. The wizard pulled her into Washington, D.C.

"Good luck," said the wizard to Rosa. "It's dangerous out there."

\* \* \*

Rosa traveled to Washington, D.C., to meet Martin Luther King Jr. in 1967.

"Where have you been?" said Martin. "I have a speech to give here in Washington, and I want you there so everything can be okay."

Martin gave his "I have a dream" speech, and Rosa watched it. "I have a dream, that one day . . ."

Because of their work, they became victorious. This means they helped people be kind to others with different skin colors.

MLK Jr. found out about the time-traveling globe, and spun it fast. The wizard spun his hand around and pulled him in.

* * *

MLK Jr. traveled back in time to Abraham Lincoln's home in Illinois in 1861.

MLK Jr. said, "Hello! I'm Martin Luther King Jr. I know about you. I'm sorry your son Edward died from pulmonary tuberculosis. You changed the world for everyone. Thank you for changing the world by freeing the slaves."

Abraham Lincoln said, "You're welcome. Thank you for changing people's lives."

The time-traveling wizard spun the globe and went into it. Abraham Lincoln went with him and landed in front of Ruby Bridges' home in New Orleans in 1980.

* * *

Abraham Lincoln saw Ruby Bridges, and she looked funny at him. "Who are you? Why are you wearing that hat?"

He said, "This is not a weird hat! I'm a president!"

"You are supposed to be dead! You're Abraham Lincoln!" said Ruby Bridges. "You said a speech to white people to persuade them to think that black people of Africa did not deserve to be treated like slaves."

Abraham Lincoln said, "You're right! But I don't know who you are!"

Ruby Bridges said, "I'm Ruby Bridges, I'm from the new times. I was born after you. I was one of the first African Americans to go to a white school."

"Thank you for telling me that!" said Abe. "I really appreciate it."

"Because you did that, you are a world changer. Now you get to spin this globe and travel through time. The wizard will tell you more," said Abe.

The wizard appeared. He said, "Spin the globe, Ruby. And my magic stick will touch it and the globe will stop. You will travel through time."

Ruby touched the globe to meet George Washington Carver. She traveled to a log cabin in Missouri in 1864.

\* \* \*

Ruby landed in front of George Washington Carver's house.

George's neighbor saw Ruby land and said, "Whoa! Who are you???"

Ruby said, "I'm Ruby Bridges. I changed the world. Did you change the world?"

George Washington Carver said, "I am an inventor. I made all kinds of stuff out of peanuts because I like peanuts. It's good. Do you want to try some?"

Ruby said, "Yes." She tries some peanut butter.

"Mmmmmm!! Good. Can I have more?" said Ruby.

George Washington Carver said, "Don't get yourself caught up too much in all this peanut butter. It might make you sick."

"Yeah . . . I think I better stop, because it will make me sick. But thank you!" said Ruby.

"How did you get here?" said George.

"I spun a magic globe and this wizard put me in it!" said Ruby.

The wizard appeared again. He said, "You've done well, and you've had good luck. George, you were also a world changer. You changed the world because you were one of the first African American inventors. You can go in the globe."

Then he spun the globe and one year later, they all gathered together in the ship again.

\* \* \*

*One year later . . .*

*Because of these world changers, all children go to school together and play together and drink from the same water fountains, and eat some peanut butter together. But don't eat too much! The end!*

# APPENDIX B

## First-Grade French-Based Language Problem Solving Group

### Shakira Moves to Georgia/*Shakira part vivre en Géorgie*

Our friend's is named Shakira. She is 8 years old. She lived in Haiti with her mom, dad, brother, and sister. Her family decided to move to Georgia because the earthquake destroyed the house and they thought it was dangerous.

*Notre amie s'appelle Shakira. Elle a 8 ans. Elle habitait à Haïti avec sa mère, son père, son frère et sa sœur. Sa famille a décidé de partir vivre en Géorgie parce que sa maison avait été détruite par le tremblement de terre. Ils pensaient qu'elle était trop dangereuse.*

Her family drives to the dock where they get on a super sonic speed boat. When Shakira gets close to the United States and she sees the ocean, she is happy.

*Sa famille va en voiture à un quai où elle s'embarque sur un bateau à vitesse supersonique. Quand Shakira s'approche des Etats-Unis et voit l'océan, elle est heureuse.*

When she arrives at the Georgia coast, her family rents a blue SUV to drive.

*Quand elle arrive sur la côte de Géorgie, sa famille loue un 4x4 bleu pour se déplacer.*

The next day, Shakira's mom takes her to school to a 1st grade class. Shakira tells her mom, "I hope to make new friends today."

*Le lendemain, la maman de Shakira l'emmène à la classe de première année. Shakira dit à sa maman : « J'espère me faire de nouveaux amis aujourd'hui. »*

---

As soon as she walks in the classroom, a boy waves to her. He says, "Hi! My name is Jarrod. What's your name?" Shakira doesn't understand his funny words. Shakira responds by saying, "Bonjour." Jarrod looks confused.

*Dès qu'elle entre dans la salle de classe, un garçon lui fait signe de la main. Il dit en anglais : « Bonjour. Je m'appelle Jarrod. Comment t'appelles-tu ? » Shakira ne comprend pas ses mots bizarres. Elle répond : « Bonjour. » Jarrod semble perdu.*

---

Jarrod tries again. He points to himself and says, "Jarrod." Then he points to Shakira and she says, "Shakira." Throughout the day, Jarrod helps her by pointing at objects and teaching her new English words.

*Jarrod essaie à nouveau. Il se pointe du doigt et dit « Jarrod », puis il pointe Shakira du doigt et elle dit « Shakira. » Pendant toute la journée, Jarrod l'aide en pointant des choses du doigt et lui enseigne des mots anglais.*

---

After lunch, Shakira is on the playground. As she is sliding on the slide, she bumps into a boy from a third grade class. She says sorry in French, but he turns around and pushes her, saying, "You don't belong here! Only English speakers belong here."

*Après le déjeuner, Shakira est dans la cour de récréation. Alors qu'elle glisse sur le toboggan, elle bute sur un garçon d'une classe de 3e année. Elle lui dit « Pardon » en français, mais il la pousse et il lui dit : « Tu ne peux pas rester ici. Seulement ceux qui parlent anglais peuvent rester ici. »*

---

Jarrod sees what's going on and runs fast to help Shakira. They tell a teacher what happened. Shakira is very sad.

*Jarrod voit ce qui se passe et il court vite aider Shakira. Ils expliquent à une institutrice ce qui s'est passé. Shakira est très triste.*

---

Her teacher talks to the class about how Shakira can only speak French. To cheer her up, they decide to all help teach her English using body language, and she helps them learn some French phrases.

*L'institutrice explique à la classe que Shakira ne parle que le français. Pour la réconforter, ils décident de tous aider Shakira à apprendre l'anglais avec le langage corporel. En même temps, elle leur enseigne des expressions françaises.*

---

By the end of the day, Shakira has made lots of new friends and has learned some new English words. She is excited about her new life. As she is waving goodbye to her new friends, she says, "Au revoir! Goodbye!"

*À la fin de la journée, Shakira s'est fait beaucoup de nouveaux amis et elle a appris de nouveaux mots anglais. Elle est contente de sa nouvelle vie. Quand elle salue de la main ses nouveaux amis, elle leur dit : « Au revoir ! Goodbye! »*

---

# APPENDIX C

## First-Grade Spanish-Based Language Problem Solving Group

### *Un equipo de fútbol mexicano con una roca mágica*/A Mexican Soccer Team with a Magic Stone

*Hay un equipo de fútbol en una escuela secundaria en México. El día de un gran partido, los miembros de equipo—Julio, Alexa, Javier, Tomás, Mike, Max, y Delia—están en la escuela.*

There is a soccer team at a high school in Mexico. The day of a big game, the team members—Julio, Alexa, Javier, Thomas, Mike, Max, and Delia—are at school.

---

*Durante la hora de almuerzo, Javier está buscando su pelota de fútbol alrededor de la escuela. Entra en un polvoriento armario para buscarla. El ve algo brillante y verde detrás de una fregona en una esquina. Él se corre sin el armario para encontrar a sus otros miembros de equipo en la cafetería.*

During lunch break, Javier is looking around the school for his soccer ball. He walks into a dusty closet to look for it. As he bends down to grab his ball, he sees something green that is glowing under a mop in the corner. He runs out of the closet to find his other team members in the lunchroom.

---

*Se reúnen en un círculo y Javier les dice sobre la cosa verde y brillante que vio. Todos ellos caminan juntos al armario. Javier cuidadosamente lo recoge y descubre que es una roca mágica. Tomás la pone en su mochila. Los miembros de equipo piensen en la roca que se encuentran el resto de la jornada escolar.*

They gather in a circle and Javier tells them about the glowing green thing he saw. They all walk to the closet together. Javier carefully picks it up and discovers that it is a stone. Javier, Julio, Alexa, Max, Delia, and Mike all touch the stone. Thomas puts it in his book bag. The team members think about the stone they found for the rest of the school day.

---

*Después de la escuela, Tomás cuidadosamente lleva su mochila al vestuario. El cambia su ropa rápidamente antes de que nadie vea la roca mágica. Después Tomas se pone su uniforme de fútbol, se pone la roca mágica en el bolsillo.*

After school, Thomas carefully carries his book bag to the locker room. He changes quickly before anyone sees the glowing magic stone. After Thomas changes into his soccer uniform, he puts the magic stone in his pocket.

---

*Julio, Alexa, Javier, Mike, Max, y Delia están esperando en el gimnasio. Inmediatamente, comienzan preguntar donde está la roca mágica. Tomás lentamente saca de su bolsillo para mostrarla a sus amigos. De repente, el entrenador, Señor Grayden, entra en el gimnasio, gritando a los jugadores para llegar rápidamente al campo de fútbol. Tomás pone la roca en el bolsillo y todos los jugadores corren al campo para el partido.*

Julio, Alexa, Javier, Mike, Max, and Delia are waiting for him in the gym. They immediately begin asking where the magic stone is. Thomas slowly pulls it out of his pocket to show his friends. Suddenly Coach Grayden comes into the gym, yelling for the players to quickly go to the field. Thomas puts the stone back in his pocket and they all run to the field for their game.

---

*El árbitro hace sonar el silbato y comienza el partido de fútbol. Javier, Delia, Max, Alexa, Tomás, Julio, y Mike comienzan a jugar el partido. ¡Después de jugar por unos minutos la roca mágica cae de bolsillo de Tomás! De alguna manera la piedra mágica vuela hacia el balón y le pega. Sorprendentemente, la roca verde cambia para combinar con los colores de la pelota de fútbol. En ese momento, Alexa patea la pelota hacia el portero. ¡Mágicamente, la pelota pasa por el portero y en la portería!*

The referee blows the whistle and the soccer game begins. Javier, Delia, Max, Alexa, Thomas, Julio, and Mike all begin playing the game. After playing for a few minutes, the magic stone flies out of Thomas' pocket! Somehow the magic stone flies toward the ball and sticks to it. To their surprise, the green color changes to blend into the ball. Just then, Alexa kicks the ball toward the goalie. Magically, the ball goes through the goalie and into the goal!

---

*¡Todo el mundo está tan emocionado que corren juntos y golpee el pecho para celebrar! Mike mira a todos y les pregunta si vieron lo que pasó. Todos los miembros de equipo de acuerdo en que la roca mágica hizo que la pelota va por el portero. Ellos se sorprenden de que la roca podría hacer algo como esto ocurre. Max le dice en voz baja a su grupo que el uso de la roca mágica es hacer trampa. Los miembros de equipo de acuerdo con Max, y todos ellos deciden que hacer trampa está mal.*

Everyone was so excited that they ran together chest bumping each other to celebrate! Mike looks at everyone and asks if they saw what happened. All the team members agree that the magic stone made the ball go right through the goalie. They are amazed that the small stone could make something like this happen. Max quietly tells his group that using the magic stone is cheating. The team members agree with Max, and they all decide cheating is wrong.

---

*Julio corre hacia la pelota y agarra la piedra mágica. Rompe la piedra mágica y lo tira a la basura. El equipo decide que Delia debe correr al árbitro y decirle que su equipo accidentalmente tocó el balón con las manos antes de que el gol anterior se marcó, para que no se merecen el punto. Todos los amigos deciden que no quieren encontrar una otra roca mágica nunca más.*

Julio runs over to the ball and grabs the magic stone. He breaks the magic stone and throws it into the trash. The team decides Delia should run to the referee and tell him that their team accidentally touched the ball with their hands before the previous goal was scored, so they should not get the point. All of the friends decide they never want to find another magic stone again.

# APPENDIX D

## Language Study

## Common Core Standards Alignment*

| Language Study Activity | Applicable Standards |
|---|---|
| **Invitations** | **Kindergarten** |
| | • SL.K.1: Participate in collaborative conversations with diverse partners about *kindergarten topics and texts* with peers and adults in small and larger groups. |
| | • SL.K.6: Speak audibly and express thoughts, feelings, and ideas clearly. |
| | • L.K.5: With guidance and support from adults, explore word relationships and nuances in word meanings. |
| | • L.K.6: Use words and phrases acquired through conversations, reading and being read to, and responding to texts. |
| | **First Grade** |
| | • SL.1.1: Participate in collaborative conversations with diverse partners about *grade 1 topics and texts* with peers and adults in small and larger groups. |
| | • SL.1.6: Produce complete sentences when appropriate to task and situation. |
| | • L.1.5: With guidance and support from adults, demonstrate understanding of figurative language, word relationships, and nuances in word meanings. |
| | • L.1.6: Use words and phrases acquired through conversations, reading and being read to, and responding to texts, including using frequently occurring conjunctions to signal simple relationships. |
| | **Second Grade** |
| | • SL.2.1: Participate in collaborative conversations with diverse partners about *grade 2 topics and texts* with peers and adults in small and larger groups. |
| | • SL.2.6: Produce complete sentences when appropriate to task and situation in order to provide requested detail or clarification. |
| | • L.2.5: Demonstrate understanding of figurative language, word relationships, and nuances in word meanings. |
| | • L.2.6: Use words and phrases acquired through conversations, reading and being read to, and responding to texts, including using adjectives and adverbs to describe (e.g., *When other kids are happy that makes me happy*.). |

### Third Grade

- SL.3.1: Engage effectively in a range of collaborative discussions (one-on-one, in groups, and teacher-led) with diverse partners on *grade 3 topics and texts*, building on others' ideas and expressing their own clearly.

- SL.3.6: Speak in complete sentences when appropriate to task and situation in order to provide requested detail or clarification.

- L.3.5: Demonstrate understanding of figurative language, word relationships, and nuances in word meanings.

- L.3.6: Acquire and use accurately grade-appropriate conversational, general academic, and domain-specific words and phrases, including those that signal spatial and temporal relationships (e.g., *After dinner that night we went looking for them.*).

### Fourth Grade

- SL.4.1: Engage effectively in a range of collaborative discussions (one-on-one, in groups, and teacher-led) with diverse partners on *grade 4 topics and texts*, building on others' ideas and expressing their own clearly.

- SL.4.6: Differentiate between contexts that call for formal English (e.g., presenting ideas) and situations where informal discourse is appropriate (e.g., small-group discussion); use formal English when appropriate to task and situation.

- L.4.5: Demonstrate understanding of figurative language, word relationships, and nuances in word meanings.

### Fifth Grade

- SL.5.1: Engage effectively in a range of collaborative discussions (one-on-one, in groups, and teacher-led) with diverse partners on *grade 5 topics and texts*, building on others' ideas and expressing their own clearly.

- SL.5.6: Adapt speech to a variety of contexts and tasks, using formal English when appropriate to task and situation.

- L.5.5: Demonstrate an understanding of figurative language, word relationships, and nuances in word meanings.

### Sixth Grade

- SL.6.1: Engage effectively in a range of collaborative discussions (one-on-one, in groups, and teacher-led) with diverse partners on *grade 6 topics, texts, and issues*, building on others' ideas and expressing their own clearly.

- SL.6.6: Adapt speech to a variety of contexts and tasks, demonstrating command of formal English when indicated or appropriate.

- L.6.5: Demonstrate understanding of figurative language, word relationships, and nuances in word meanings.

### Translation Charts

### Kindergarten

- SL.K.1: Participate in collaborative conversations with diverse partners about *kindergarten topics and texts* with peers and adults in small and larger groups.

- SL.K.6: Speak audibly and express thoughts, feelings, and ideas clearly.

- L.K.1: Demonstrate command of the conventions of standard English grammar and usage when writing or speaking.

- L.K.5: With guidance and support from adults, explore word relationships and nuances in word meanings.

- L.K.6: Use words and phrases acquired through conversations, reading and being read to, and responding to texts.

### First Grade

- SL.1.1: Participate in collaborative conversations with diverse partners about *grade 1 topics and texts* with peers and adults in small and larger groups.

- SL.1.6: Produce complete sentences when appropriate to task and situation.

- L.1.1: Demonstrate command of the conventions of standard English grammar and usage when writing or speaking.

- L.1.5: With guidance and support from adults, demonstrate understanding of figurative language, word relationships, and nuances in word meanings.

- L.1.6: Use words and phrases acquired through conversations, reading and being read to, and responding to texts, including using frequently occurring conjunctions to signal simple relationships.

### Second Grade

- SL.2.1: Participate in collaborative conversations with diverse partners about *grade 2 topics and texts* with peers and adults in small and larger groups.

- SL.2.6: Produce complete sentences when appropriate to task and situation in order to provide requested detail or clarification.

- L.2.1: Demonstrate command of the conventions of standard English grammar and usage when writing or speaking.

- L.2.5: Demonstrate understanding of figurative language, word relationships, and nuances in word meanings.

- L.2.6: Use words and phrases acquired through conversations, reading and being read to, and responding to texts, including using adjectives and adverbs to describe (e.g., *When other kids are happy that makes me happy.*).

### Third Grade

- SL.3.1: Engage effectively in a range of collaborative discussions (one-on-one, in groups, and teacher-led) with diverse partners on *grade 3 topics and texts*, building on others' ideas and expressing their own clearly.

- SL.3.6: Speak in complete sentences when appropriate to task and situation in order to provide requested detail or clarification.

- L.3.1: Demonstrate command of the conventions of standard English grammar and usage when writing or speaking.

- L.3.5: Demonstrate understanding of figurative language, word relationships, and nuances in word meanings.

- L.3.6: Acquire and use accurately grade-appropriate conversational, general academic, and domain-specific words and phrases, including those that signal spatial and temporal relationships (e.g., *After dinner that night we went looking for them.*).

### Fourth Grade

- SL.4.1: Engage effectively in a range of collaborative discussions (one-on-one, in groups, and teacher-led) with diverse partners on *grade 4 topics and texts*, building on others' ideas and expressing their own clearly.

- SL.4.6: Differentiate between contexts that call for formal English (e.g., presenting ideas) and situations where informal discourse is appropriate (e.g., small-group discussion); use formal English when appropriate to task and situation.

- L.4.1: Demonstrate command of the conventions of standard English grammar and usage when writing or speaking.

- L.4.5: Demonstrate understanding of figurative language, word relationships, and nuances in word meanings.

### Fifth Grade

- SL.5.1: Engage effectively in a range of collaborative discussions (one-on-one, in groups, and teacher-led) with diverse partners on *grade 5 topics and texts*, building on others' ideas and expressing their own clearly.

- SL.5.6: Adapt speech to a variety of contexts and tasks, using formal English when appropriate to task and situation.

- L.5.1: Demonstrate command of the conventions of standard English grammar and usage when writing or speaking.

- L.5.5: Demonstrate an understanding of figurative language, word relationships, and nuances in word meanings.

### Sixth Grade

- SL.6.1: Engage effectively in a range of collaborative discussions (one-on-one, in groups, and teacher-led) with diverse partners on *grade 6 topics, texts, and issues*, building on others' ideas and expressing their own clearly.

- SL.6.6: Adapt speech to a variety of contexts and tasks, demonstrating command of formal English when indicated or appropriate.

- L.6.1: Demonstrate command of the conventions of standard English grammar and usage when writing or speaking.

- L.6.5: Demonstrate understanding of figurative language, word relationships, and nuances in word meanings.

| | |
|---|---|
| **Language Problem-Solving Project** | Because of the unique nature of language problem solving, the standards addressed will vary based on students' and teachers' chosen projects. It is likely that applicable standards will include many of those listed above, along with standards pertaining to reading, writing, and research. |

***Please Note:*** The standards identified are those most closely related to the teaching of language. Language study also involves exposure to a variety of texts, writing assignments, and problem-solving activities. The standards listed here indicate exposure to these concepts during particular language study activities; *mastery* of these standards will not occur right away. The formative assessment data collection tools throughout this text will help educators determine when students have mastered the content.

# WORKS CITED

Ada, Alma F. 2001. *Gathering the Sun: An Alphabet in Spanish and English.* New York: Rayo.

———. 2004. *I love Saturdays y domingos.* New York: Atheneum Books.

Allen, JoBeth. 2007. *Creating Welcoming Schools: A Practical Guide to Home–School Partnerships with Diverse Families.* New York: Teachers College Press.

———. 2010. *Literacy in the Welcoming Classroom: Creating Family–School Partnerships That Support Student Learning.* New York: Teachers College Press.

Allen, JoBeth, Jennifer Beaty, Angela Dean, Joseph Jones, Stephanie Mathews, Jen McCreight, Elyse Schwedler, and Amber Simmons. 2015. *Family Dialogue Journals: School–Home Partnerships That Support Student Learning.* New York: Teachers College Press.

Andrews, Larry. 2001. *Linguistics for L2 Teachers.* Mahwah, NJ: Lawrence Erlbaum.

Barman, Charles R., and Michael Kotar. 1989. "Teaching Teachers: The Learning Cycle." *Science and Children* 26 (7): 30–32.

Black, Paul, and Dylan William. 1998. "Assessment and Classroom Learning." *Assessment in Education: Principles, Policy, and Practice* 5 (1): 7–74.

Campbell, Linda M., and Bruce Campbell. 2008. *Mindful Learning: 101 Proven Strategies for Student and Teacher Success.* 2d ed. Thousand Oaks, CA: Corwin.

Cazden, Courtney B. 1972. *Child Language and Education.* Boston: Houghton Mifflin.

Christensen, Linda. 1996. "Whose Standard? Teaching Standard English." In *Language Development: A Reader for Teachers*, edited by Brenda M. Power and Ruth S. Hubbard, 209–13. Upper Saddle River, NJ: Prentice-Hall.

Curriculum Implementation Unit: Teaching and Learning Branch. 2002. *A Guide to Productive Pedagogies: Classroom Reflection Manual.* Brisbane, QLD: Education House.

Delpit, Lisa. 1994. "Acquisition of Literate Discourse: Bowing Before the Master?" *Theory into Practice* 31 (4): 296–302.

———. 1995. *Other People's Children: Cultural Conflict in the Classroom.* New York: New Press.

Dyson, Anne H. 2001a. "Donkey Kong in Little Bear Country: A First Grader's Composing Development in the Media Spotlight." *The Elementary School Journal* 101 (4): 417–33.

———. 2001b. "Where Are the Childhoods in Childhood Literacy? An Exploration in Outer (School) Space." *Journal of Early Childhood Literacy* 1 (9): 9–39.

Dyson, Anne H., and C. Genishi. 2005. *On the Case: Approaches to Language and Literacy Research.* New York: Teachers College Press.

Dyson, Anne H., and G. Smitherman. 2009. "The Right (Write) Start: African American Language and the Discourse of Sounding Right." *Teachers College Record* 111 (4): 973–98.

Fasko, Daniel. 2000. "Education and Creativity." *Creativity Research Journal* 13 (3): 317–27.

Fecho, Bob. 2004. *Is This English? Race and Culture in the Classroom.* New York: Teachers College Press.

Freire, Paulo. 1972. *Pedagogy of the Oppressed.* Translated by Myra Bergman Ramos. New York: Continuum. (Original work published 1968.)

Garza, Carmen L. 2000. *En mi familia/In My Family.* San Francisco: Children's Book Press.

Gebhard, Meg, Ruth Harman, and Wendy Seger. 2007. "Reclaiming Recess: Learning the Language of Persuasion." *Language Arts* 84 (5): 419–30.

Gee, James P. 1989. "What Is Literacy?" *Journal of Education* 171 (1): 18–25.

———. 2011. *Social Linguistics and Literacies: Ideology in Discourses.* London: Routledge.

Genishi, Celia, and Anne H. Dyson. 2009. *Children, Language, and Literacy in Diverse Times.* New York: Teachers College Press.

Giovanni, Nikki. 2008. *Hip Hop Speaks to Children: A Celebration of Poetry with a Beat.* Naperville, IL: Sourcebooks.

González, Lucia. 2008. *The Storyteller's Candle: La velita de los cuentos.* New York: Lee and Low.

González, Norma, Luis Moll, and Cathy Amanti, eds. 2005. *Funds of Knowledge: Theorizing Practices in Households, Communities, and Classrooms.* Mahwah, NJ: Lawrence Erlbaum.

Gutiérrez, Kris D. 2008. "Developing a Sociocritical Literacy in the Third Space." *Reading Research Quarterly* 43 (2): 148–64.

Heath, Shirley B. (1983) 1996. *Ways with Words: Language, Life, and Work in Communities and Classrooms.* New York: Cambridge University Press.

Henderson, Anne T., Vivian Johnson, Karen L. Mapp, and Don Davies. 2007. *Beyond the Bake Sale: The Essential Guide to Family–School Partnerships.* New York: New Press.

Hicks, Deborah. 1995. "Discourse, Learning, and Teaching." *Review of Research in Education* 21 (1): 49–95.

hooks, bell. 1989. *Talking Back: Thinking Feminist, Thinking Black.* Brooklyn, NY: South End Press.

———. 2004. *Skin Again.* New York: Hyperion Books.

Hudley, Anne H. C., and Christine Mallinson. 2011. *Understanding English Language Variation in U.S. Schools.* New York: Teachers College Press.

Janks, Hilary. 2010. *Literacy and Power.* New York: Routledge.

Knapp, Peter, and Megan Watkins. 2005. *Genre, Text, Grammar: Technologies for Teaching and Assessing Writing.* Sydney: University of New South Wales Press.

Maslow, Abraham H. 1943. "A Theory of Human Motivation." *Psychological Review* 50 (4): 370–96.

McKissack, Patricia. 1986. *Flossie and the Fox.* New York: Dial Books.

Medina, Jane. 1999. *My Name Is Jorge: On Both Sides of the River.* Honesdale, PA: Wordsong.

Nieto, Sonia. 2002. *Language, Culture, and Teaching: Critical Perspectives for a New Century.* Mahwah, NJ: Lawrence Erlbaum.

———. 2009. *The Light in Their Eyes: Creating Multicultural Learning Communities*, 10th anniversary ed. New York: Teachers College Press.

Nilep, Chad 2006. "'Code Switching' in Sociocultural Linguistics." *Colorado Research in Linguistics* 19: 1–22.

Patterson, Francine. 1987. *Koko's Kitten.* New York: Scholastic.

Raschka, Chris 1998. *Yo, Yes!* New York: Orchard.

———. 2000. *Yo, Yes!* (Video). Norwalk, CT: Weston Woods Studios.

Renzulli, Joseph S. 1997. *How to Develop an Authentic Enrichment Cluster.* Storrs: Neag Center for Creativity, Gifted Education, and Talent Development, University of Connecticut. Retrieved from http://gifted.uconn.edu/schoolwide-enrichment-model/authentic_enrichment_cluster/.

Rymes, Betsy 2009. *Classroom Discourse Analysis: A Tool for Critical Reflection.* Cresskill, NJ: Hampton.

Schleppegrell, Mary J. 2010. "Supporting a 'Reading to Write' Pedagogy with Functional Grammar." In *Language Support in EAL Contexts: Why Systemic Functional Linguistics?*, special issue of *NALDIC Quarterly*, edited by Caroline Coffin, 26–31. Retrieved from http://oro.open.ac.uk/25026/1/.

Secret, Carrie. 1998. "Embracing Ebonics and Teaching Standard English." In *The Real Ebonics Debate: Power, Language, and the Education of African American Children*, edited by T. Perry and Lisa Delpit, 79–88. New York: Beacon.

Solsken, Judith, Jerri Willett, and Jo Anne Wilson-Keenan. 2000. "Cultivating Hybrid Texts in Multicultural Classrooms: Promise and Challenge." *Research in the Teaching of English* 35: 179–211.

Treffinger, Donald, and Scott Isaksen. 2005. "Creative Problem Solving: The History, Development, and Implications for Gifted Education and Talent Development." *Gifted Child Quarterly* 49 (4): 342–53.

Van Sluys, Katie. 2005. *What If and Why? Literacy Invitations for Multilingual Classrooms*. Portsmouth, NH: Heinemann.

Vasquez, Vivian. 2014. *Negotiating Critical Literacies with Young Children*, 10th anniversary ed. New York: Routledge.

Wheeler, Rebecca, and Rachel Swords. 2004. "Codeswitching: Tools of Language and Culture Transform the Dialectically Diverse Classroom." *Language Arts* 81 (6): 470–80.

Woolfolk, Anita 1998. *Educational Psychology*, 7th ed. Boston: Allyn and Bacon.